A TRULY LOYAL SUBJECT:

An Account of the Life of George Brown and the Founding of Canada

by Vincent Marquis, B.A., B.Ed., M. Min., O.C.T.

© Copyright Vincent Marquis, 1997, 2006, 2017, 2020

All rights reserved. No part of this work may be reproduced or used in any form by any means - graphic, electronic, or mechanical, including photocopying, scanning, recording, information storage and retrieval systems, without written permission from the author-publisher.

Acknowledgements

I would like to express my appreciation and gratitude to those who encouraged me and helped me in various ways in completing this account of one Canada's most controversial Founding Fathers, foremost of whom are my wife and children. Many others, both locally and nationally, encouraged me to do something about recording some parts of the neglected historical heritage of our nation with respect to the influence of Christians and Christian values on its past. Special thanks to those who read, corrected errors, and provided critique of the drafts.

Any errors, inaccuracies, or misinterpretations are entirely my responsibility.

Dedication

To Sir Leonard Tilley, who gave the nation of Canada its motto:
"He shall have Dominion from sea to sea." (Psalm 72, verse 8)

Forward to the Teacher/Adult Reader

There was a time when the world seemed, and perhaps was, a much simpler place. Canada, it was assumed by its English-speaking inhabitants, was basically a British country, and so was loyal to the Monarchy and proud to be part of the great British Empire. For French-Canadians, Canada was home, and the only fatherland they knew. They simply accepted British rule as fact born of necessity, and even developed a kind of backdoor loyalty to British government, if not to the Crown and British traditions.

The Native Peoples, of course, knew and felt little, if any, of this. The concept of "Canada" did not exist for them. They lived their lives in the lands their ancestors had inhabited in the ways they had been taught for generations. But for them as well the world was changing, and they would find themselves engulfed in the white man's advancing world, to the great detriment of their own. Some would adapt to some degree; some would eventually abandon the old ways altogether; all would be affected deeply, for better or for worse. All the founding peoples of this great country contributed to the culture and society we enjoy today. Many others came to join them later, and made, as do those arriving today, their own unique contributions.

Canada has never been a static country, and it has adapted to a great many innovations, sometimes willingly and sometimes not. Out of this ethos, we have created a number of near-myths about the nature of this country. These myths constitute the current dominant mindset of the popular version of Canadian history taught in the public education systems, and Canadians have generally bought into this stereotype, believing it to be true "because everybody says so."

This modern public interpretation of history depicts Canada arising out of a series of political manoeuvres born of economic necessity and political ambition. The Christian roots of this country now lie largely buried. One purpose of this book is to dispel some of the mist that has veiled an essential part of the truth from our eyes. Another is to put the unification of Canada, called "Confederation" in its history, in a larger perspective than the very cursory version delivered in the scanty Canadian History education offered in the country's elementary and secondary schools. A third is, hopefully, to simulate interest in the fascinating history of their country in young Canadians, and perhaps even in some older readers who have never learned much about the "story within the story".

When people reduce the world to a two-dimensional stage and say that man has body and mind, but no soul or spirit, all decisions, events, policies, and movements based on high principles become incapable of proper analysis. Something must be imputed to men's motivations that will render them more realistic. Unfortunately, the results of such (un)scientific interpretation are caricatures that hide reality.

Canada once was a decidedly Christian country, insofar as any country ever has been. Many of its leaders not only publicly professed to be Christians but lived privately as Christians. Many of their pronouncements and actions reflected their convictions. If they did not often publicly state these convictions, it was because they *assumed*, usually rightly, that these were common values that most public figures would accept. Values such as honesty, integrity, loyalty, fidelity, civility, and temperance were extolled, if not always faithfully modelled by the men in leadership.

In this book, we will be taking an unconventional look at the impact that personal Christian faith had in public life in the pre-Confederation period, particularly through the story of George Brown. Brown's historical reputation has suffered since his death in 1880. Historians have generally treated him as a harsh, sharply bigoted, arrogant, proud, bad-tempered, intolerant, and overly ambitious man. He certainly had his faults, as do we all, but it is my conviction that Brown has suffered unduly in comparison to the undeniable attractiveness of Sir John A. Macdonald. Brown had the historical misfortune of being "Old Tomorrow's" arch-opponent during those crucial years, and Macdonald's sun continues to leave all his contemporaries in its shadow. His unfortunate rivals have been totally eclipsed.[1]

The unfortunate part of this for George Brown is that his extraordinary role is now all but forgotten, and his character has been caricaturized by Macdonald's witticisms as "that covenanting old fellow", or worse. It is interesting to note that all of Brown's serious biographers, from the first, Sir Alexander Mackenzie, 1882, to the last and definitive biographer, J.M.S. Careless, 1959, 1963, have found an admirable, and sometimes even warm, affectionate person beneath the forbidding exterior left to public memory by the heat of intense political battle and the verdict of historians. It is also interesting to note that Brown's opponents recognized a peculiar high-mindedness in him that often irked and even infuriated them in its uncompromising pursuit of truth and justice, sometimes even to his own hurt. In our postmodern tolerant society we

---

[1] In recent years, Macdonald's reputation has taken quite a hit. His racism towards indigenous peoples, Métis, Blacks, and Asians has stimulated demands that statues honouring him be removed from public places and that history books tell this side of the story. Others reply that Macdonald was a man of his time, no worse than most others in such attitudes and treatment of minorities. George Brown appears quite progressive in comparison.

easily equate strength of conviction with arrogance, for we arrogantly allow no other standard by which to see it as anything else.

Preface to the Student

Canada is a great country. Its land mass is the second largest in the world. Its population is not of the same order, but it is a prosperous land that has one of the leading economies of the world. Canada is also a well respected country around the world, and is known as a peaceful and peace-loving place. It is thought to be a generous land because it has so often helped other people in their times of disaster, or when soldiers have been needed to help warring people stop fighting.

People of other nations once would grouped Canada among "Christian countries", part of the world often called "the West". Part of being one of these nations was the idea of being generous and peace-loving. Within Canada itself there are still many Christians. In 2019, more than half of its population still thinks of themselves as "Christian" in some sense, and they are often very involved in helping suffering people around the world. There are also still Christians holding office in Canada's Federal, Provincial and Municipal governments, but it is no longer safe to assume that Canada is a Christian country, and there is no "official religion" in Canada.

Culturally, politically, economically, socially, and religiously, many things have changed in Canada in the last 200 years. There is much debate as to whether some of these things have been good, although of course many have been very beneficial for everyone. As for the change in the way people see religion, and especially the Christian religion which was once so influential in Canada, things are vastly different from what they were at the time of the story told in this book.

Let us think about some of the good changes first. For example, 200 years in ago in Canada almost no roads existed, and none of the ones that did were paved. For travelling, there were no trains, cars, or planes. Trips took a very long time compared to today, no matter how one travelled – by walking, by horse, by wagon, by sailing ship, or by canoe. Steam ships were a very new invention. There were no telephones and no post offices. There was no electricity to light homes, run machines, or give heat. There were no firemen or police officers. There were no public schools, and few private ones. There were no computers, no Internet, TV, or radio. In fact, all of these things were unimaginable to people two centuries ago. We would probably all agree that we enjoy having these things and wouldn't know what to do without them.

In fact, 200 years ago, Canada was not even a country, as we know it. Canada was a British colony, or rather, a number of British colonies, or provinces, each separate from the others. Before that, most of Canada had been controlled by the French in the centre and east, the British in the north, and the Natives in the west. In 1763, France surrendered its part of Canada, called **New France**, to the British after being defeated by the British in the Seven Years' War of 1756-1763.

You can probably see by now that Canada was a very different country in the past from what it now is. People lived differently both because of what they didn't have and what they *did* have that we no longer have, or that we can no longer find very easily. One of the things that was easy to find during much of the past was openness towards Christian belief. Most people who lived in or came to Canada would have called themselves Christians. Few people then thought it would be a good idea to stop people from talking about God in public, or to make fun of Christians or their beliefs. The idea that you could make good laws without consulting God's law in the Bible first would have been thought absurd by a great many of the leaders of our past. To make laws that went *against* God's law would have been thought not only foolish, but immoral, and dangerous indeed.

For many Christians in Canada in the 21st Century, it is easy to be concerned with the kinds of laws and leaders that have gained power with an agenda to change Canada into a nation that is less and less Christian. You will be able to make your own decisions and judgments about these matters as you learn and grow.

In this book about George Brown, we will find that his Christian beliefs and principles were very important in helping him make decisions and live in a way that can inspire others. He was certainly not alone as a leader and statesman in that regard. The country itself would readily have accepted being called "a Christina country". Most of its leaders would have said and really believed that they were Christians.

The chief character of this true story, George Brown, was far from perfect, but he knew that Jesus had died for his sins and had trusted Him to forgive those sins. He believed that, when he died, Jesus would welcome him into His Kingdom.

Introduction

The story told in this book took place during the time when Canada was not yet an independent nation. The life of the main character, George Brown, began soon after Canada's last war with the United States had ended in 1814. It ended seven years after Prince Edward Island, the last autonomous British colony of North America except Newfoundland, had joined the Dominion of Canada in 1873. Before telling that story, and the story of *Confederation,* in which he played a major role, we should recall some of the main facts about Canada's history up to the time when this story begins.

Before the 1600s, there were no permanent European settlements in Canada. The first Europeans to try to colonize Canada seem to have been the Vikings around 1000 CE. These daring adventurers did not succeed. According to the old Norse Sagas, the Native Peoples drove them out.

In the 1400s, before the official European "discovery" of America and Canada in the 1490s[2], we know that fishermen from Portugal and France, and perhaps from England, were fishing on the Grand Banks east of Newfoundland and Labrador. These fishermen also came ashore in Newfoundland and Labrador to dry their fish before sailing home. Some may even have wintered there occasionally if they had waited too long before the bad weather set in, causing many terrible winter storms at sea.

These fishermen traded for furs with the natives and sold them for a good profit back in their home countries. Then the Kings of England and France got involved by sending officially approved explorers to lay claim to the land[3] and the wealth that might be found there! In fact, it seems

---
[2] Of course, the real discoverers of Canada were the First Nations, who had been on "Turtle Island" (North America to Europeans) for thousands of years.

the fishermen tried to keep their governments out of the picture, and succeeded for many years. They spread tales of great sea monsters and terrible creatures to frighten away others.

Few Europeans thought much about these unknown places, or that the "wild people" living there needed missionaries sent to them. Most of the Europeans at first thought they had actually reached islands close to India in Asia, which is where they had really aimed to go. They did not treat the "Indians"[4] like fellow human beings, but instead enslaved them, killed them, or forced them to become subjects of their King.

The French were the first Europeans to seriously colonize Canada. Jacques Cartier's and Roberval's attempts in the 1530s and 1540s were paid for and largely pushed forward by the French Protestants, called *Huguenots*. These people suffered persecution in mainly Catholic France, and hoped to establish a place in the new world where they would be free to worship and live according to their religion in freedom. Jealousy among the merchants and nobles of France played a role in ending these early attempts to settle in Canada, but the severe climate probably was the greatest discouragement to those settlement efforts.

It was finally in 1608 that Samuel de Champlain founded the city of Quebec and the colony of New France. Quebec grew very slowly at first. It was seen as a base for operating the fur trade with the natives, and for sending missionaries to them. Only in the 1660s did the French government finally take direct control of the colony to try to make it

---

[3] It is now quite astonishing to us how one group of nations could think they had a right to just arrive in someone else's country or territory and claim they now owned it because the first inhabitants were "savages".

[4] "Indians" is the term used by the European settlers for the Native Peoples in those centuries, and up until recent times. It came from the original mistake of thinking they were close to India in Asia. If the term is used in our story, it is not meant to be derogatory or imply that the First Nations are inferior in any way. It is a reflection of the language used in the 1800s.

strong enough to survive on its own and pay its way. The program of expansion by the French brought about conflict with the English colonies that had grown up to the south along the Atlantic coast.

When there was war in Europe between the French and the British, there was war in America between the colonies of these countries. In these wars, the much smaller French population defended itself well, with much help from France. Finally, in the Seven Years War of 1756-1763, which actually began in 1755 in North America, England sent a powerful army and fleet to conquer Quebec, which fell to them in 1759. In 1760, the last French army in Canada surrendered, and control of Canada passed to Britain from France for good, as was recognized in the Treaty of Paris in 1763.

At first, Canada as a British colony was still basically French-speaking, although ruled by English officials. In 1775, Britain's American colonies to the south along the Atlantic coast revolted against Britain. The Americans sent two armies to invade Canada in that year. One captured Montreal while the other attacked Quebec. The Americans hoped the French-Canadians would join their revolt. They did not, and French-Canadian militia troops even helped repel the American attack on Quebec City.

The Americans eventually won their independence from Britain in 1783 with the help of France and even some support from Spain. Many thousands of Americans had remained loyal to Britain during the war, or had not actively helped the revolution. Over 30,000 of these left the new United States to escape persecution or even death and came to New Brunswick or Quebec.

Those who moved into the part of Quebec west of Montreal did not want to live under the domination of a French Catholic majority. They asked Governor Simcoe to get Britain to give them their own territory with its own local English-speaking government. In 1791 Britain did this. The British Parliament passed the Constitution Act in that year, separating Quebec into two colonies, Upper Canada in the west and Lower Canada in the east. New Brunswick and Nova Scotia were already separate colonies. The Far West, which we know as the Prairies, was under the control of the Hudson's Bay Company, a British Corporation involved in the fur trade.

The two "Canadas" grew as more settlers arrived. Another war with the United States from 1812-14 showed Britain that protecting her colonies in "British North America" would become more and more difficult as the United States grew and became more powerful. Britain strengthened Canada's defences, and the population in Upper and Lower Canada continued to grow.

By the 1830s, many of the people in both Canadas felt that Britain's colonial governments were oppressive and preventing them from having any say in their own affairs. A small group in each province had all the advantages and benefits. These elite groups gave all the best positions to their friends, controlled the Legislatures, and had the governors' favour. In 1837, a number of circumstances brought these resentments to a boil in both Upper and Lower Canada. In Lower Canada, violent revolt broke out in November. The clashes between British troops and French-Canadian *Patriotes* went on sporadically until March 1838. By then most of the rebel leaders, including Louis-Joseph Papineau, had fled to the United States. Others had been captured, of whom some were hanged and some imprisoned.

In Upper Canada, a brief revolt broke out in December, led by William Lyon Mackenzie, a newspaper publisher and the leader of the Reform Party. This revolt was swiftly defeated by loyal militia, and Mackenzie and some other leaders also fled to the United States. When the British Government heard about these revolts, it decided to send a special envoy as Governor General to investigate the causes and recommend changes to the way the two Canadas were governed. The British government of the time was *Whig*, or Liberal. The new Governor-General was Whig too. He was John Lambton, Lord Durham, and his impact in Canada's history would be great, even though he stayed a mere eighteen months.

Durham quickly recognized that a return to the old status in the Canadas would not be acceptable. It was time to allow the people to elect representatives to Legislatures which would have real power. It was time to allow more people to vote.[5] This would mean that the governors should no longer ignore the Legislatures if they did not like what they said or did. It also would mean that the governors should not overrule the legislators, even when they did not agree with the laws they made.

But Durham wanted to go even farther than this. He wanted the Governors to select their Council of special advisors, or *Cabinet*, from among the elected representatives of the *Legislature* (or *Parliament*). This would ensure that the people's voice would be heard and that their desires would be carried out. This would avoid any further need for rebellion.

---

[5] Only adult males 21 years of age and older were allowed to vote in those days. They also had to own some property worth enough to pay a minimum amount of tax on. Lambton lowered the amount of tax paid to allow a man to vote.

Durham also though about the population of the Canadas. He realized that as long as there was a large number of French-speaking, Catholic people, there would always be the possibility among them of dissatisfaction with Protestant Britain's rule. That might eventually mean that they might demand independence, or cause more rebellion or internal tension. The best way to end these future problems would be by removing the cause. But he did not want to use force to compel the French-Canadians to give up their language and religion. Nor was it conceivable to expel the French-Canadians from Canada like Britain had done to the Acadians in Nova Scotia in 1755. Such measures would certainly cause a very bloody rebellion. Nor did he want to arrest people or pass unjust laws.

He believed that the best and safest way to solve the "French-Canadian problem" was to swamp the French-Canadians with English-speaking immigrants and surround them with a dominant English culture. Gradually, he thought, the "habitants" would lose their language and give up their religion in order to gain power and wealth and become equal to the dominant English.

To make sure this happened more quickly, he recommended that Upper and Lower Canada be united into one single colony to be called the Province of Canada. In the Parliament of this "United Province", the English members would dominate the French members, and so Lower Canada, or Canada East as it would now be called, would be controlled by Englishmen from both the West and the East.

Not all of Durham's recommendations were followed. At that time, the Colonial Office, the department of the British government in London,

England was in charge of colonies. Some of Durham's ideas were partially put in place, some were completely accepted, and others were not tried. For example, the British government agreed that it was best to unite Upper and Lower Canada into one single province with only one Parliament. But rather than allow the English-speaking people of Canada West to eventually have more members of Parliament than the mostly French-speaking people of Canada East, the government gave the two halves the same number of members. The leaders in London thought that this would prevent "separatism" in Canada East (Quebec). This decision would be increasingly resented in the West as their population grew rapidly and then surpassed that of Canada East. This resentment also had a religious side, as the mostly Protestant West grew angry about being controlled by the mainly Catholic East.

It is at this point that George Brown arrived in Canada. Let us now tell his story, and that of the contribution he made to solving this bitter problem.

Chapter 1: From Edinburgh to New York

George Brown was born on November 29, 1818, in Alloa, Scotland, not far from Edinburgh, Scotland's capital. His mother was Marianne Brown, wife of the prosperous merchant, Peter Brown, George's father. The Browns were proud of their heritage on both sides of the family. Peter's ancestors were hard-working, free, and proud folk who had raised themselves up by their own efforts. Marianne's distant ancestors included great people from both England's and Scotland's past, people like John of Gaunt (the "Black Prince"), King John, and King Edward I!

George already had two older sisters when he was born, and he would have two younger sisters and a younger brother too. Sadly, his parents also lost three boys as babies, but they were a happy family most of the time. The Brown family were devoted Presbyterians, but, unlike some of Scotland's Presbyterians, they believed that each local church should govern itself. They strongly opposed government involvement in church affairs, or making a church, even the Presbyterian Church of Scotland, an official religion supported by the government in any way.

At the same time, they believed it was wrong for churches to get involved in politics. Peter Brown taught his children that, to be free, a man must decide his religious beliefs for himself. No one should ever be forced to believe or go to a church because the government says so. Not only that, but governments should not support any particular church with money or give it special privileges, because that also makes it more difficult for people who cannot accept the state church's teaching or way of doing things. These ideas of religious liberty and *the separation of the church and the state* would play a very important role in George Brown's life when he rose to a position of leadership in Canada.

George grew into a boisterous, fun-loving young man. He was intelligent, tall, strong, and quick-witted. His father wanted George to go to university to become a respected and learned professional. Like any good parent, his father wanted his son to have opportunities he would have liked to have had, but didn't.

Although Peter Brown had not gone to university, he was well-educated for that time, and he was very well read. As a prosperous merchant, he was well-respected in Edinburgh, and he knew many important people. George met many of these people too, for as he grew up he often accompanied his father on trips and to meetings. His father also invited many people home to talk about theology, literature, politics, and new ideas. Marianne Brown, George's mother, shared many of their ideas and concerns, and she also encouraged George.

Eventually, George convinced his parents not to send him away to university, even though he had graduated from the Southern Academy of Edinburgh at the top of his class. His high school's Headmaster, or Principal, said that, "This young gentleman is not only endowed with high enthusiasm, but possesses the faculty of creating enthusiasm in others."(1)[6] He was probably remembering some of George's pranks as he said this.

George entered the family business. Soon he travelled to London and other places in Britain, learning about trade and commerce. As the oldest living son, and because of his good humour, his friendly nature, and his intelligence, he was a favourite in the family. He and his father were very close, talking about everything together. George greatly

---

[6] Numbers in brackets refer to Endnotes at the back of the book. These Endnotes tell which source in the Bibliography provided the citation or information referred to, and where it can be found in that source.

respected and admired his father, and his father came to rely on him and respect him more and more too.

In Britain in the 1830s, a great many changes were taking place in society, industry, religion, and politics. In 1832, when George was 13, a great reform of Britain's Parliament, which met in London, was made. This was achieved only after much struggle, including many demonstrations, marches, petitions, and finally after a great election win by the Whig Party, which Peter Brown supported in Edinburgh. There was a giant celebration of this great event in Edinburgh in August 1832, which George could well have taken part in as part of the large crowd of over 60 000 who either participated or watched. Other changes were being pushed for and successfully obtained as well. These included changes in the way local governments, such as the one in Edinburgh, were run. Peter Brown became involved in municipal politics at this time.

In spite of all their success and the many activities they were engaged in, if someone had asked the Brown family what was the most important thing in their lives at this time or later, he might have been very surprised at the answer. Many people then, and now, would expect to hear answers like, "Success! Money! Prestige! Respect! Friends!"

The Browns thought that these were good things, but to them there was something much more important - their Christian faith. "Family prayers, Sunday-school teaching for George, charitable work among the poor for his mother and elder sisters, all were an essential part of their lives.... And certainly, his whole life was influenced by the strong faith that supplied almost core and foundation for the unity of the Brown family."(2) They believed and would later fight for the principle that everyone should serve God first, as his conscience commanded him, and then serve the state. This, they held, is the foundation of freedom for all men, and governments must never interfere with it, nor must any man interfere with any other man in this.

Some people think that being "religious" or Christian is dull and dreary. Furthermore, they think that religious people of the 19th century, or Victorian Era, were very stern, humourless people who never had any fun and were always finding things wrong with others. No doubt, there are now "religious" people like that, and there were then. But not the Peter Brown family of Edinburgh.

When he was 18, George joined a club called the "Philo-Lectic Society of Edinburgh". They would meet to discuss and debate important questions of what we call today "current events." One evening in early 1837 George was giving a talk on Phrenology, a popular idea that people's personality and character can be told by the shape of their head, especially by the locations of the bumps! As silly as this may sound to us, some people took this very seriously at the time, just as others take astrology or palm-reading seriously. When a famous phrenologist named Bryson challenged George in the meeting, saying that he didn't know anything about it and so should not talk about it, George silenced him by admitting that he didn't have the right bumps on his head to be as wise as Mr. Bryson, but that the Phrenologist's wisdom and intelligence bumps didn't seem to have done him any good either. This remark resulted in uproarious laughter at Brown's quick wit.

The good times for the Brown family ended when Peter Brown's business fell on hard times. As a trustee for some public accounts, Peter had got some public money and some of his business money mixed up. When a depression hit Scotland in 1837, Peter had inadvertently lost track of the city's money. He had not been dishonest, or taken it for himself; he had made an error and now sought to set it right. To keep him out of trouble with the law, some of his friends lent him the £2 500 (about $12,500 at that time, but much more in today's money) to pay to the city of Edinburgh's accountant.

Peter was devastated, and with the depression his business declined so badly that he could not repay his friends, even though they told him they were in no rush to get their money back. Peter believed that, in honour, he should do all he could to set things right, but that he would no longer be able to do so if he remained where he was. After much thought and prayer, and talking together as a family, he decided to move to America, and George would go with him. There they would start up again, and bring the rest of the family over as soon as they could afford a decent place for Marianne, the girls, and young Gordon in which to live.

They sold everything and kept enough to pay for the trip and get them started in America, as well as to allow the rest of the family to live till they could send for them. With the rest, they paid some of their debt to their friends. Then, in April 1837, Peter and George Brown sailed for America aboard the American brig *Eliza Warwick*.

What was it like to cross the Atlantic Ocean by sailing ship? The idea of it might seem adventuresome and exciting to us. Today most people cross the ocean by airplane in a few hours, but in 1837 everyone who wished to travel between Europe and North America had to go by ship.

Most ocean-going ships in those days were sailing ships. Few steam ships were made to sail on the ocean. Steam engines had a bad habit of often breaking down, and so even the ocean-going ships had to carry enough masts and sails to make sure they could get to their destination if the engine failed.

The *Eliza Warwick* was overloaded with passengers, almost all immigrants from Britain to the United States. Therefore, it did not make good time crossing the Atlantic. In one storm it met, the waves washed right over the decks of the ship. Fortunately, no one was lost.

Most people travelling by ship in those days paid only for the trip itself. Only well-to-do people paid for a ready-made bed and their meals as well. Everyone else had to either buy whatever they needed for the trip themselves in port before the trip began or they went without, unless someone kind and generous shared with them during the voyage. The Browns bought their own provisions for the trip. George did the cooking for them! After a longer than the usual passage that took 10 weeks, they arrived in New York City on June 12, 1837.

Chapter 2: From New York to Toronto

New York City in 1837 was not yet the great city of millions of people that it is today. Nevertheless, it was a large and rapidly growing city for that time, just as the United States was a dynamic country whose population, wealth, prosperity, and power were increasing rapidly.

The Browns settled in the city, and Peter Brown began a dry goods business[7], just as he had in Scotland. By good management and careful saving, the Browns were soon making a profit, and their business grew steadily, in spite of the depression. A year after they had arrived, Peter and George were able to bring across the rest of the family, not second-class as they had come, but first-class, with all expenses paid and comfortable beds and good food! They were all together again, and they soon settled down as a happy family in New York.

As the business kept on increasing, George became more and more an equal partner. Peter sent him on business trips up the Hudson River, into western New York State, and, eventually in 1843, even into Canada. George was responsible for making good deals purchasing materials from suppliers, as well as finding new stores to which they could sell their goods. While the business was doing well, the sisters started a school for girls.

Meanwhile, Peter Brown began writing articles for a newspaper that was published by immigrants for immigrants from Britain. This newspaper, the **Albion**, was popular. Peter discovered that he enjoyed journalism so much that he became a regular contributor to the paper.

---

[7] "Dry goods" meant what we would now call "hardware" and equipment.

Peter and his son, George, also decided that they did not particularly like the American political system. Both of them believed that the British system was far better. The Americans were too radical. They found that full democracy, with every man having the right to vote no matter how illiterate or uninformed, was dangerous. Peter wrote that a society based on this kind of government would be at the mercy of unscrupulous manipulators who could talk people into almost anything.

Peter found himself having to defend his ideas, as there was a large movement in America for full democracy, and putting the ordinary people in charge of business, banks, and politics. In the Presidential campaign of 1840, the candidates seemed to vie with each other to see who could prove that he had had the simplest and humblest beginnings in life, and who would be most like "just folks". It was dubbed the "Log-Cabin" campaign.

Praising Britain in comparison to the United States while living in the U.S.A. was not a way to be popular. There was much anti-British feeling in America. Britain was still seen as the U.S.'s main potential enemy. America and Britain had already fought two wars, the War of Independence, 1775-83, and the War of 1812, 1812-14. There were border disputes between the U.S. and Britain over Maine and, in the early 1840s, in the "Oregon Country" in the Far West.

Peter even wrote a book to prove that Britain's constitution and government was superior to the United States'. The book was entitled, **The Fame and Glory of England Vindicated.** Peter enjoyed writing this book so much that he decided to sell his dry goods business and begin his own newspaper, specifically for immigrants from Britain living in New York. He called it the **British Chronicle**, and it began publication on July 30, 1842.

This newspaper proved successful, as many of the new immigrants from Britain enjoyed receiving news from the old country regularly, and reading articles about themselves and the affairs of the British immigrant community. Before long, the Brown newspaper was being sold even in Canada West among the people there who were of British, and especially of Scottish origin.

In fact, so many people from Canada West began reading the **British Chronicle**, that Peter began to include items about events in Canada, and wrote sympathetically about the Reform movement in Canada. But the affair that became the dominating news in the paper had to do with a religious story.

In 1842 a great debate erupted in the Presbyterian Church of Scotland, the church of which the Browns had always been members. The debate began in Scotland, but eventually spread to both America and Canada. Although the question was rather complicated, we will try to state it simply here, without getting bogged down in details.

Basically, there were two groups in the church with very different views about how much a Scottish government official, or someone with a lot of power in the Church, should be able to control who could be a minister in a local church. Some people said that such officials could force a congregation to accept a minister even if they did not want that particular man, but had another preference. These people were called "Intrusionists." The other group said the congregation should decide who could minister, and outside officials, or even a powerful local person who had influence with the church's top leaders, should not be able to force a congregation to accept someone of whom they did not approve. This group was called the "Non-Intrusionists."

In May, 1843, the Church of Scotland split over this issue. The Intrusionists outvoted the Non-Intrusionists in the Church's General Assembly. The Non-Intrusionists believed the Church had become corrupt because it was willing to allow possibly corrupt and godless people to appoint ministers who might also be corrupt. They therefore withdrew from the Church of Scotland to begin the Presbyterian Free Church.

George was now the publisher of the **British Chronicle**, and as such was in charge of building the paper's circulation. As he had with the earlier business, he travelled to do this. In the spring of 1843 he visited Canada's leading English-speaking cities. In June, in Toronto, some of the Presbyterian Free Church leaders offered George and his father $2500 and a guaranteed minimum readership if they would move their paper to Toronto and support their movement.(4)

George returned quickly to New York. After much discussion, the family, minus sister Jane, now married, decided to move to Toronto where their admiration of Britain would be welcome. The last issue of the **British Chronicle** was issued on July 22, 1843. On August 18, 1843, the first issue of their new, Canadian paper, called the **Banner**, appeared in Toronto.

Chapter 3: Publisher of the Globe

As of the year 2020, Toronto is the fourth largest city in North America with a metropolitan population of about six million people. In 1843, it was a bustling little city of about sixteen thousand. In some ways, it was still half frontier town. It did not stretch very far north from Lake Ontario, except along Yonge Street, which was the major "highway" heading towards Lake Simcoe and Orillia.

There were still regular British soldiers stationed in Toronto, although not a large number. The people of Toronto believed their city would be great one day. They worked hard, and, for a small city, many businesses were established there. There was talk of railway building. The Lachine Canal had opened the St. Lawrence to allow large ships to come all the way to Lake Ontario from Montreal. But Montreal was, at that time, as it would be for a long time still, the largest and most important commercial and industrial city of Canada.

Britain's flag, the Union Jack, was a welcome sight to the Browns as they arrived by steam-boat from Niagara Falls, New York. They could feel almost at home here. In fact, George felt quite at home. The young man of 24 years had high expectations, as he told his father. "The country is young. There are few persons of ability and education. There is no position a man of energy and character may not reasonably hope to attain...."(5) Peter was content to know that they had reached their final destination and would move no more.

The **Banner** was an unusual kind of newspaper. It was half religious and half political. Peter edited and wrote the religious articles. George handled the political side, for he was already acquainted with some

Reform Party ministers of the government from his previous trips to Canada. Politics and religion were very much mixed together in that era.

The **Banner** often spoke out against the Tory government's support of the Anglican religion over others. Religion in those days meant any one Christian denomination. They wrote, "We know that power alone proceeds from God, the air we breathe is the gift of His bounty, and whatever public right is exercised from the most obscure elective franchise [i.e., the poorest person with the right to vote] to the king upon his throne is derived from Him to whom we must account for the exercise of it...."(6)

As important as the religious affairs shaking the Presbyterian Church in Canada were, George found that he was more and more being drawn into the political affairs of Canada West. In this area too he found there was an important struggle taking place, and he felt he needed to be able to give full attention to it and provide good information and guidance to the people of Canada West. Therefore, after less than a year in Canada, he decided to launch a second newspaper, devoted to public affairs and politics. He would call this new paper, which would be his, not his father's, the **Globe**. One day, long after he died, it would become the renowned **Globe and Mail**.

It was not that Toronto had no "secular" newspapers already. In fact, there were an astonishing number of newspapers for such a small city. Every political group seemed to have its own newspaper. Newspapers of that time did not pretend to be neutral or try to be objective. They took sides on issues, often without much hesitation, and used very strong language. If people called one another the same kinds of names today as they used to then in their hot political debates, they might get sued, and newspapers would not allow their articles to appear without removing the offensive remarks.

This reflects the truth that people generally took politics very seriously and got very emotionally involved. They often had strong convictions about things, especially when they involved religion and morals, and so they spoke out strongly. Also, many issues of the time involved religious questions. People were not embarrassed to say where they stood on such things and to tell their opponents that they were wrong in no uncertain terms. Therefore, it is no surprise that even in a "secular" newspaper like the **Globe** George Brown and then later Gordon Brown used their position as editor to talk often about religion when discussing major issues.

The **Globe** had the encouragement and support of some of the top men in the Reform Party. There was already a Reform paper in Toronto, the **Examiner**, but the party's leaders were unhappy with it. They thought that it would be good to have a second one with a strong, intelligent, and fresh perspective such as they felt this new young man could provide. Therefore, they even lent George money to start the **Globe**, which he was able to quickly repay.

From the very beginning, the **Globe** gained recognition as a strong new voice in Canada West's affairs. George Brown quickly established a reputation as a sharp, forceful, very persuasive writer. He was found to make few mistakes in his facts, and based his opinions on those facts. He was a skilled debater, and was a master at dissecting his opponent's arguments.

This meant that he rapidly made many friends, gaining the respect of Reform supporters, often at the expense of the **Examiner**. Even Tory supporters bought the **Globe** because it usually had the most recent news reported most accurately, and, in many cases, even before the other papers. But they also bought it because, increasingly, they could not ignore what Brown was saying. He often stated what were, or would soon be, the official views of Reformers.

It was thus that George Brown's new paper became the most successful and widely read newspaper in Toronto and Canada West within one year of starting publication. This made George Brown the most successful publisher in Canada West, and therefore someone who was a power to reckon with. He had only been in Canada for two years, and his statement to his father about "a man of energy and talent" attaining high position already seemed on the way to fulfilment.

Chapter 4: Voice of Reform

It was in the struggle for *responsible government* that George Brown and his **Globe** would first make their mark and establish themselves as the most powerful voice of Reform policies in Canada.

Let us see what those policies were as explained in the **Globe** by George Brown in an editorial called "The Great Conservative Party" on Sept. 18, 1847. He began by saying that the Conservatives, who had by then governed for 3 years, stood for nothing except keeping power to themselves. He continued:

> Go to the street and ask the first man you meet "what party do you belong to?" If he tell you he is a Reformer, and you ask him What his party wants? he will tell you at once "We want Responsible Government, out and out-we want the ministry [government ministers] to be consulted on every step taken by the Provincial Government; we want an increase in the number of Parliamentary Representatives-national common school education [public schools], free from sectarianism [denominational religious teaching]- national grammar schools-perfect religious equality-penny postage, under Provincial control-the sale of the clergy Reserves - Jury Reform - Assessment Reform - and the abolition of the navigation laws; we are opposed to all connection between Church and State, and to grants of public land or money to any religious sect whatever; we desire to throw open King's College [Canada West's university in Toronto that favoured Anglicans but was supported by the provincial government. It later became the University of Toronto.] to all Her Majesty's subjects alike, and to banish tests[8] and the teaching of theology from the University; we want to encourage manufactures, agriculture, railroads, and internal improvements of every character; we want our country to be great and prosperous."

---

[8] "Tests" did not mean exams in courses. It referred to "testing" a person's religious views to make sure they fit the kind of students that the college preferred to admit.

We do not need to know what all these things concern at this point. We **can** point out that several of these Reform policies referred to specifically religious influences in politics.

Much is made today, for instance, of the point Brown made when he said, "we are opposed to all connection between Church and State..." Almost all modern politicians, whether Liberal, Conservative, NDP, or Green in Canada, or Republican or Democrat in the United States, would completely agree with this. But what is usually forgotten is that what Brown and the Reform Party of the 1840s in Canada meant by this, and what this has come to mean in our very different society in the 21st Century are actually quite different.

When the Reformers of the 1840s spoke about separating Church and State, they did not mean keeping religion out of public life, or penalizing people for publicly declaring what they believe, or forbidding people to pray, sing hymns, or share the Christian Gospel in public. Yet this is what this has come to mean in the present era. George Brown and many of the politicians of his time would be astonished and appalled by the way our courts, law-makers, and media have twisted this basically very good idea.

It is important to realize what these things used to mean in comparison to what they have now come to mean. By understanding the difference, we can gain a better insight into what Canada used to be like as compared to what it is now. We might better appreciate our own past and find valuable things there that should be restored to our society, if at all possible. Or, if they cannot be restored, perhaps they could help us be more truly tolerant of differing religious views than we really are. Strangely, in some things, especially the increasing bias against Christianity and Christian values in education and public life, our culture has actually become religiously *less* tolerant than it was around the time of Confederation, although, of course, many aspects of life have improved greatly for minority groups.

What did "Separation of Church and State" mean in 1847? The Reformers of that day, many of whom, like George Brown, were Christian believers, looked back at 300 years of British and European history where rulers had told their subjects to what church they should belong. They had even punished those who had disobeyed, sometimes killing or imprisoning them, or forcing them to leave the country. They remembered that terrible wars had been fought over religion, and millions of people had died as a result of these wars-in Germany, in France, in Holland, in England, and in some smaller countries.

They also saw, in England, Scotland, and Ireland, the injustice of the government favouring one religion over another. Having moved to Canada to start a new life and hopefully be free from some of those old quarrels and problems, they found instead that some of the same injustices had been continued. They wanted these ended. They never would have suggested that Christianity should be eliminated from the country's life, or its schools. They expected that the government would simply be neutral, not about people being Christians, but about what denomination, or church, people preferred to belong to.

That was what Mr. Brown was talking about when he wrote this comment about King's College in Toronto in the **Globe** of Nov, 13, 1847:

> "Young men in a Christian land, with Christian parents and Christian Ministers, do not go to college to learn the truths of Christianity. That must have been learned before they went there. But it will ever be the business of the patrons of such institutions to fill the Chairs [professors' jobs] with men who will teach every

> science as Christians ought, both in the mode of doing it, and by the example they set before the students."

Reformers felt that the College should not be teaching any one church's theology. It was a school paid for by all the taxpayers, not just the favoured Anglicans. But it should be faithful to the truth of Christianity. Canada was a "Christian land," and its leaders at every level should be held accountable for not living and leading as Christians ought. This was the view of George Brown, and of his newspaper, the **Globe**, and George Brown and the **Globe** were "the voice of Reform" in Canada West in many people's minds.

Chapter 5: Government Mouthpiece

In the election of December, 1847, the Reform Party won a majority in Canada West, and a strong minority of their friends, *Les Rouges*, were also elected in Canada East. In addition, the new Governor-General, Lord Elgin, was committed to the idea of responsible government. The Reformers took power. Their leader in Canada West, Robert Baldwin, became Prime Minister, and he made the **Globe** the official Reform newspaper.

Now George Brown was an even more important man in Canada West. During the election campaign he had actively participated to help Hincks, one of the key Reform leaders, get re-elected, even though Mr. Hincks was away in England and unable to get back in time to conduct his own campaign. Brown was also being invited to speak at more and more meetings as a Reform leader.

Like many western Canadians, Brown was excited about the new government and expected it to take action on most of their policies in the next four years. The Tories, however, were not prepared to sit back quietly and simply allow responsible government to work. They still dreamed of regaining power and ruling without putting everything before Parliament for approval. They still hoped to hold on to special privileges for the many of their number who had been benefiting from the Anglican and Presbyterian Churches' special status.

They tried to use fear to stir up the people against the Reform government. When the government passed a law called the *Rebellion Losses Bill* stating that those who had lost property in the rebellions of 1837-8 should be paid back, the Tories raised the cry of "Treason! Disloyalty to Britain!" Their fanatical followers rioted in Montreal and burned down the Parliament Buildings on April 25, 1849, even threatening Lord Elgin himself. Other disturbances occurred in Toronto and Kingston. The **Globe** office was attacked, and the Browns' home in Toronto had windows broken. George himself was threatened by anonymous hate letters.

The Reformers waited out the turmoil, realizing, as Brown wrote, that these were the last desperate convulsions of a dead idea. He was right. Once the Tories realized that their attacks had failed to scare the government or turn the majority of people against them, the disturbances ceased.

In June 1848, George was asked to take part in an investigation of the conditions at the penitentiary in Kingston. He was glad to do this, for he had been brought up to believe in the dignity of all human beings as God's creatures. This belief also made him a hater of slavery, and moved him and his whole family to become involved in helping black slaves who escaped from their masters in the southern United States and succeeded in reaching Canada.

The reports of conditions in the prison at Kingston were shocking. The Warden, Henry Smith, was suspected of being cruel and vicious with the prisoners. There were suspicions that he had used money sent to run the prison and provide for the needs of prisoners to enrich himself. His fifteen year-old son had been given a job as cook, although he spent much of his time tormenting some of the inmates. He had even, it was said, made a bow and shot several convicts with blunt arrows, causing one of them to lose an eye.

From July 1848 to February 1849, the special Commission conducted its investigation in Kingston. George Brown was the Commission's secretary. He dominated the inquiry and wrote its final report. He was also responsible for many of the recommendations made to improve things.

The evidence of wrong-doing was overwhelming. Brown was disappointed that the government did not fire Warden Smith right at the beginning. Instead, they waited until Brown and the other commissioners angrily insisted that Smith *had* to be dismissed, even though things had continued badly at the prison even after the investigation began. Many of the Commission's recommendations were not implemented, although a few were.

This was Brown's first occasion of disappointment with the government. Another outcome of this episode was that Smith, who was from Kingston, complained to John A. Macdonald, the Conservative MP for Kingston, that the Commission was fixed against him from the start.

Macdonald did not bother to look at the overwhelming evidence against Smith. Instead, he defended Smith by attacking the Commission, and Brown especially, as conducting a smear campaign against a good man and his family. Hincks, the Attorney-General of the government, defended the Commission, but never bothered to defend Brown against Macdonald's charge that he had been out to get Smith from the start. Once again, Brown was left with an uneasy feeling about the government.

Another concern that arose during this time was a movement to annex Canada to the United States. This movement was started in Montreal by Tory businessmen, who had earlier accused the Reformers of treason! For Brown, this proved that the Tories were more concerned about regaining power and staying rich than being loyal. The reason these men said that Canada should join the U.S. was so that Canada could become prosperous like the U.S. It so happened that there was a short depression at this time. When it cleared up, they stopped talking about annexation.

But another group picked up the idea. These were radical Reform supporters in Canada West who had hoped that the Reform government of Baldwin from Canada West and Lafontaine from Canada East would bring in U.S.-style democracy by reforming the constitution. They wanted every man to have the right to vote instead of limiting the vote to only those owning property. As well, they wanted every important official, such as judges and sheriffs, as well as law-makers, to be elected.

Brown and the Reform leaders saw these men as much more dangerous than the Tory annexationists. They could stir up a lot of support in Canada West and split support for the Reform Party. Brown accused them of trying to turn Canada into a republic like the U.S. He wrote a long series of articles in the **Globe** explaining why the British style of government was better. He sounded like his father, Peter, in his book **The Fame and Glory of England Vindicated**.

Once more, George was somewhat disappointed by Baldwin's failure to deal strongly with these people. He felt *they* should have written some of this defence, and not leave the whole job to him. These maverick reformers organized themselves into a powerful new group called the *Clear Grits*. This meant that they believed themselves to be true to real Reform principles while they considered Baldwin, Hincks, and their supporters compromisers. The Clear Grits soon had several members of Parliament on their side, and their own newspaper, the **North American**, which spent a lot of time attacking the **Globe** and its editor-in-chief, George Brown.

At this point, in 1850-51, a whole series of events then occurred which completed Brown's disillusionment with the Baldwin-Lafontaine government. The common link in all these issues was religion.

Chapter 6: 1850 - Year of Disillusionment

As we have seen, the Brown family were strong supporters of freedom of religion. In those days, they called this idea "voluntarism." They thought that it was wrong for a government to prefer one denomination over another, or to treat one denomination better than another, or give any denomination special privileges.

However, the Anglicans and the Roman Catholics had received special treatment, while the Presbyterians also had some minor benefits. There were two main ways in which these privileges had been gained by these religious groups, land and schools. The land question went all the way back to 1791.

In 1791, Sir John Graves Simcoe, the first Lieutenant-Governor of Upper Canada, had made a secret agreement with the Anglican and Presbyterian Churches that only they would have support from special tracts, or sections, of land. The new Constitution Act which had just come into force in Canada in that year had said land should be set aside to support the establishment of churches in newly settled areas. These land tracts were known as *Clergy Reserves*.

Because of Simcoe's agreement, nobody but Anglicans and Presbyterians ever got any of this land. Therefore, the Methodists, Baptists, and other Christian churches in Upper Canada had to pay all their own costs to build and maintain churches and pay their ministers, or clergy. In the question of schools, the first schools in Upper Canada were paid for by the parents of the children who went there. But in 1808 the first law was passed that allowed people in an area to start a grammar or elementary school. The Anglicans arranged for the religious instruction at the schools to be Anglican. Other people had to accept that their children would be taught Anglican ideas even if they were not Anglicans. Since people were not obliged to send their children to school, this was not then a major issue.

In May 1850, Brown and most Reform supporters expected the government to pass a law to abolish the Clergy Reserves. As Canada's second Prime Minister after Confederation, Sir Alexander Mackenzie, wrote in his biography of Brown in 1882:

> "...it was impossible for the liberals [Reformers] of Canada West to consent to any compromise on this question which would admit of any church, with the national sanction, express or implied, assuming the status of an established or dominant church. The demand was imperative that all denominations of Christians must stand equal before the law."(7)

Parliament had moved back to Toronto after the burning of the Parliament Building in Montreal in 1849. When there was no mention of the Clergy Reserves being abolished in the Governor-General's opening address, Brown hoped that this did not mean the government had decided to do nothing.

Within a month it became clear that the government was divided on what to do. Some of its members wanted the lands sold to the public. Prime Minister Baldwin, an Anglican himself, wanted the lands divided up among the churches, each getting a part according to its size. His close friend and ally, Lafontaine of Canada East, did not want the lands touched at all. As a Roman Catholic from Quebec, he wanted to protect the position of the Catholic Church. If church lands in Canada West were made public, he expected a demand to do the same thing with the Catholic Church's lands in Quebec. He did not want to have to fight a political war over that, for he did not think he could win.

The government decided to delay things by sending a special request to the British Parliament in London, England. Because these lands had been set aside in the Constitution of 1791, they said, they did not have the power to touch them without London's permission. In June they did pass some resolutions that supported the idea that the Reserves should be disposed of "with justice for all churches." For George Brown and many Reform supporters, this was a disappointment. Brown, however, considered it better than nothing and advised that they should wait for further action in the next session of 1851.

In June 1850, Francis Hincks introduced a new Education bill called the *Common School Bill*. Most of this law was in line with what Reform supporters wanted. It set up a non-sectarian public school system for all Canada West. No denomination would teach its doctrines, although there would be Bible instruction, moral teaching, and prayers in the schools, and teachers were expected to be good, moral people according to Christian standards.

There was one problem with this law, as the **Globe**'s editor and many Reform supporters saw it. It allowed the Catholics to set up their own schools wherever they felt they wanted one, provided they had at least 12 families who asked for it. It allowed Roman Catholics to set their taxes aside to support the Separate Catholic schools. For the politicians in power, they worried that if they did not give Catholics this privilege, the numerous Catholic voters would not support them in the next elections. The Catholic Bishops and priests exerted a lot of influence on these voters to pressure the politicians.

For Brown, this was an unacceptable giving in to pressure from Catholic Liberals in Canada West. Allowing this kind of exception, he said, would eventually open the door for other denominations to demand the same treatment. In fact, if Catholics were to be allowed, why should not others be? It is interesting that this very argument was unsuccessfully used by modern Ontario's private Christian schools and Jewish schools to claim the right to government support for their schools in the 1990s.

As we have seen, Brown and the mass of the Reform Party's members wanted a common, public school system to which everyone would send their children, and for which everyone would pay by taxes. In the **Globe**, Brown declared, "We think the principle thus admitted [by allowing one denomination to have its own schools supported by taxes] strikes at the roots of our whole system of national education. It is the entering wedge."(8)

Despite the opposition of Brown and many supporters of the government, the Common Schools Act became law and the Catholics had their schools. This was one more disappointment for George Brown in a mounting string of them. In the **Globe**, it was becoming more and more difficult for Brown to support the government, and it seemed to George that the government ministers had less and less respect or regard for him and true Reform principles.

This became even more clear when a government member who was sitting in the public gallery of Parliament with two young lady friends one day accused George's reporter at Parliament of insulting him when the reporter asked him to be quiet so he could hear the speeches which he had to report on in the next issue of the **Globe**. The next day, the Reform MP got Prime Minister Baldwin and Parliament to publicly reprimand the reporter. All the newspapers withdrew their reporters till the end of the session, feeling that it was unacceptable for Parliament to punish someone trying to do his job. It seemed clear to George Brown that the government no longer respected the **Globe** or appreciated all he had done for them.

Another incident was much more personal to Publisher-Editor Brown of the **Globe**. Just before Parliament ended its sitting for 1850, John A. Macdonald again brought up the Penitentiary inquiry. He called George Brown a vicious scoundrel, and the Commission was accused of malice, improper procedure, and distorting evidence.(9) The government ministers, who had called the Commission into being and who had asked Brown to serve on it, said nothing to defend Brown, and only half-heartedly defended the Commission. Although they defeated Macdonald's motion to set up a committee to look at the Commission's work, they left Macdonald's charges open. This wounded Brown personally and definitely sent him a message that he was no longer seen as a useful friend by the government ministers.

The closing episode of this period embroiled George Brown and the **Globe** firmly in a damaging and divisive controversy he at first tried to avoid. It involved the sharp divisions between Roman Catholicism and Protestantism. Although Brown did not ask for this fight or start it, he ended up being identified as the chief spokesman for the Protestant side. He also ended up making up his mind about the government.

The quarrel started in Rome. The Pope decided that the Roman Catholic Church in England needed to be formally organized, which it had not had since King Henry VIII had founded the Anglican Church in 1534. He therefore divided the English branch of the Catholic Church into dioceses, each of which is simply an area under a Bishop's authority, and he named the Archbishop of Westminster head of it all and made him a Cardinal.

It may be hard for us today to understand why this should start a major religious dispute, and why it should have any importance in Canada. But in 1850 English Protestants still remembered the days when Popes told Kings and Emperors who should be Bishops. In fact, the Pope's power had once been so great that he could control Kings themselves by telling their subjects not to obey them.

Pope Pius IX, who was then Pope, was suspected of wanting to wield that kind of power again. He claimed that Catholics should obey him rather than the King if he commanded them not to obey the King. This was exactly the kind of thing that "voluntarists" like George Brown believed was very wrong – that religious leaders should interfere in political life, and vice-versa.

When the Pope organized the English Catholic Church, he did it without consulting Queen Victoria or anyone else. Protestants of all denominations considered his action an aggressive intrusion into English affairs. They believed that the Pope was making a statement that he still held religious power over England, even though most English people were not Catholics.

Another reason Protestants were sensitive about this was that a number of leading Anglicans had recently joined the Catholic Church. There was a whole "back to Catholicism" movement going on among well-educated young Anglicans centred at Oxford University led by a brilliant ex-Anglican priest named John Henry Newman.

This uproar from England crossed the Atlantic to Canada. Many of the religious newspapers debated it hotly, as well as a number of the **Globe**'s secular competitors. Meanwhile the **Globe** remained strangely silent. George Brown did not wish to be drawn into a debate he thought would only cause anger and division between Catholics and Protestants in the Reform Party.

He only broke the silence when a Roman Catholic government minister from Canada East challenged him, almost as a joke, to publish a long essay by England's Roman Catholic cardinal on why the Pope's action was right. Brown thought about it and replied that he would accept the challenge, as long as the minister did not mind if he wrote his own reply to the cardinal at the same time. The minister, M. Tâché, accepted this reply.

Brown's reply to the Cardinal caused a furore. The very thing he did not want happened. Catholics and Protestants argued ferociously, and the Catholics never forgot that George Brown became the primary spokesman for the Protestants in the hot debate. **The Globe's** participation in this debate drove another wedge between Brown and the government.

We might wonder whether Brown regretted having got involved after he had at first resolved not to. Long afterwards, in 1871, in a long letter to a group of leading Catholic Liberals of Ontario, he tried to explain that he had never hated Catholics or denied their right to believe as they liked. He recognized that there were real and strong differences between Catholics and Protestants. He declared that Reform's fight to separate religion and politics had been for everybody's benefit, including Catholics:

> "I deny not that in this protracted contest words were spoken and lines were penned that had been better clothed in more courteous guise. But when men go to war they are apt to take their gloves off; and assuredly if one side struck hard blows the other was not slow in returning them.....I ask those of you who can do so, to carry your minds back to the position held by Catholics in times gone by, and

say whether any other section of the people of Upper Canada has such good reason to rejoice in the banishment of sectarian issues from the political arena, and the perfect equality of all denominations now so firmly and so happily enjoyed, as have the Catholics of Ontario."(10)

He ended this peace-making letter by asking them not to look at who wrote it, but at the truth of what it said. They should decide whether the Conservatives, who stood for special privileges for certain Protestants, or the Liberals, who stood for equality for all, had treated Catholics better and deserved their support.

Chapter 7: From Journalist to Politician

The year 1851 would prove pivotal for George Brown. His political opinions and his life would take a new direction. The change in Brown's life would result in the beginnings of a change in the life of the country as well.

The first major event of the new year, which George celebrated in the warm company of his family, as he usually did, was a decision to take the plunge into politics as a candidate in a *by-election* in the *riding* of Haldimand. Having watched politics from the sidelines for many years, Brown decided that his views could best be forwarded by being in the arena himself.

The campaign was not a happy experience for George. Although he was the official Reform Party candidate, he received no active support from any of the government ministers or members. His opponent was William Lyon Mackenzie, the old rebel leader for 1837. Mackenzie had returned to Canada following and *amnesty* granted by the government in 1849.

Haldimand was Clear Grit country, and Brown was identified by Clear Grit supporters as a compromised "ministry man." Mackenzie was not a Clear Grit, but he had the reputation of being a radical like them. The result was a loss for Brown.

George did not like to lose at anything, and he was not accustomed to losing either. He found the loss hard to bear, and he was wounded by the almost total neglect he had felt from the government during his campaign. Little did he then know that his loss and his alienation from the government would actually prove a blessing in disguise in the long run. Many of those who voted against Brown were Catholics. His opponents gloated that he had got what he deserved. Brown indignantly replied in the **Globe** that it was a sad day for the country if a man was disqualified for Parliament because of his religious beliefs. It seems that this lesson has not been learned yet even now.

Parliament began its 1851 session on May 20. On June 30, 1851, Robert Baldwin stunned everyone by announcing his immediate resignation as Prime Minister and MP. A conscientious, honest, pleasant, and competent man, he was utterly worn out by the years of quarrelling and dealing with less honest people than himself. His old co-leader and long-time friend and partner, Lafontaine, soon resigned as Liberal (Rouge) leader for Canada East. This left Hincks in charge of the West and Morin in charge of the East. Brown liked neither of them, and neither of them liked Brown.

Brown finally broke with the Reform government when Hincks, the new Prime Minister, attacked the **Globe** in his first Prime Ministerial speech because Brown had denounced the government's allowing churches to set up tax-exempt corporations to run special schools, hospitals, and other properties. From this point on, the **Globe** was free to criticize whom it pleased as it pleased. George Brown would stand by his principles, saying "even if it means ten years in opposition".

To Brown's mind, the biggest issue needing speedy resolution was the Clergy Reserves question. He and his father had helped found The Anti-Clergy Reserves Association. Tory bullies attacked George and his father at a peaceful mass meeting in July 1851. The next day, the same thing happened again, and the bullies tried to break down the locked doors of St. Lawrence Hall, where the meeting was being held. Only when British troops arrived did the mob disperse.

This kind of thing did not scare the Browns. George gave his stirring speech anyway. He said that State control of the Church had created "pride, intolerance and coldness." He blamed the terrible religious wars of centuries past on the desire of rulers to force people to believe their way. He continued:

> "....when I observe the degenerating effect which it has ever had on the purity and simplicity of the Gospel of Christ, turning men's minds from its great truths, as a religion of the heart, to the mere outward tinsel, to the forms and ceremonies on which priestcraft flourishes; when I see that at all times it has been made the instrument of the rich and powerful in oppressing the poor and weak, I cannot but reject it utterly as in direct hostility to the whole spirit of the Gospel, to that glorious system which teaches men to set not their hearts on this world, and to walk humbly before God."(11)

Late in July an amazing political shift occurred. Brown had been predicting it for weeks in the **Globe**, although the newspapers controlled by the Reform government and radical Clear Grits had been denying it right up to the last minute. The Clear Grits joined the "moderate Hincksite" Reform government in return for a share in the *Cabinet* posts. This was a clear hint that an election would soon follow. Hincks and his new allies wanted to go quickly to the voters to get their support. The election was called in mid-November for December-January.

Brown owned a large tract of land in Kent county, near Sarnia. He had friends in the area, one of whom was Alexander Mackenzie, Canada's future Prime Minister from 1873 to 1878. They invited him to run in their riding as an Independent Reform candidate, promising him their full support, and help in the campaign.

Remembering his bad experience in Haldimand, Brown hesitated for weeks. Finally, he decided "to go in" and give it his best effort. He now realized that there was no one in Parliament to strongly defend the principles he believed in and thought best for the country. Either he accepted defeat, or he did his duty and entered politics to fight for them himself. He decided that the time had come to fight. He had not sought politics; rather, it had sought him out. He would actually have preferred to stay at the **Globe** full time.

Chapter 8: George Brown, the Man

George Brown won his campaign and became the Member of Parliament for Kent. He belonged to no party, but sat as an Independent Reform member, as he would for some years. At the **Globe**, Brown's brother Gordon was taking over as the Managing Editor to run the paper day by Day, for George would now be away much of the time "politicking." As long as we was in politics, George would not be able to be fully involved with his newspaper. Gordon became an equal partner.

George still had a very important say in the paper's overall direction. He usually got his way in deciding the big questions, such as what line of opinion to take in editorials, and in expanding or reordering the business side. He still wrote some of the editorials too when he had the time, and his important speeches were always reported on, and often reprinted in full or in large part.

The **Globe** continued to be the most important newspaper in Canada West, even though it no longer had government approval. Often when people enter politics, their principles either change or get "watered down" by compromise. For the sake of gaining and keeping power people will often do and say things they would not otherwise. It seems that the power of being able to control and manipulate people and events to suit oneself takes over from conscience and principle in many politicians' minds and wills.

George Brown was in politics for the next sixteen years as a member of Parliament. No one was ever able to pin the slightest hint of corruption on him. He held to his principles even when this made him hated and unpopular, even when his life was in danger from enemies. Through all this, he was to have a major impact on the country, and play a leading role in creating a new and greater Canada in Confederation.

Just like today, politics in the mid-1800s was not a polite business. Nor was it gentle. Opponents called one another nasty names. Violence was common around election-time, and sometimes in between. People tended to overlook a politician's personal problems unless they were so bad they could not be ignored.

Some men, for example, used their political position to make money through knowing where to invest money ahead of time. Others drank heavily, sometimes even attending Parliament drunk. The newspapers generally did not publicize these things even if they knew, as long as they did not get in the way of a man usually doing a good job as an MP.

George Brown was never known to be drunk, although he did not totally abstain from alcoholic beverages. Very few men did in those days. He was a supporter of *temperance*. Although he invested and made a lot of money, he never used his position to do this, or to get money from the government for himself. He was a faithful husband and devoted father and never acted improperly with women.

As a Christian, he believed that it was important to live out his faith, not just talk about it. Brown held that real Christians were followers of Christ by free choice, not by compulsion because of culture, tradition, or laws. He believed that people who were Christ's followers would freely do the kinds of good things Christ wanted them to do. It was not true Christianity to use fear or force of any kind to get people to do what might look like the right thing.

George Brown firmly believed that all religions, or denominations, should have the same access to education and legal rights and social benefits. It was wrong for governments to grant special favour or status to any one sect. Therefore, it was wrong for governments to make laws allowing any one sect to have special schools or hospitals with government approval and freedom from taxes.

Almost always when he spoke on these issues, Brown upset Roman Catholics. Some of them thought he must actually have horns, since he was such a heretic and ally of the devil. They actually believed that only an atheist could hold such opinions. The Roman Catholic Church was *the* true church in their eyes. It deserved special rights. It should use its power to push politicians to give them special status in every way possible.

Physically, George Brown was a big man, powerful and impressive. He stood six feet, two inches, or 188cm. He was not overweight, although he was known to have an enormous appetite. He was always on the go and had enormous energy. He was known to work so much and so hard that he could exhaust many others before he was worn out.

In his election campaign in Kent, he would speak four or five times a day for eight hours or more, not counting travel over terrible roads by carriage or horse. He was considered a good-looking man. In his younger years he had red hair, and he grew long side-burns in middle age. He had a deep voice that, when he warmed up in a speech, carried well in the days without microphones and Public Address systems. He could hold a crowd of several thousand spell-bound for hours, even in a hot, stuffy hall. When he was speaking he did not stand still, but was known to beat the air with his arms as he made his points.

Brown was also a successful business man. He was constantly seeking ways to improve the **Globe** and stay ahead of his competition. The **Globe**'s circulation grew steadily. It became a daily newspaper in 1853 with 6000 subscribers. By 1856 it had 18,000 subscribers. Toronto's population at this time had just passed 50,000.

In addition to the **Globe**, Brown invested in land near Sarnia. He cleared land and sold the wood and land to settlers who came in on the new railroad from Hamilton to Windsor. He built mills, and established a village called Bothwell. He supported the building of railroads, although he opposed the corruption often involved in the deals between politicians and railroad men. He also disapproved of the loans the municipal and Provincial governments gave to the railroad companies without guarantees.

In his home life, George was always close to his parents and sisters. Catherine, the youngest sister, was especially close. George was devastated when she was drowned in a train wreck on October 15, 1857, near Syracuse New York. His father, who was with her, survived with minor injuries. George was depressed for weeks afterwards.

George married in November 1862 when he had almost turned 44. His wife was the daughter of a Scottish publisher named Thomas Nelson. The Nelson company become one of the most successful publishing houses of Britain.

George's marriage was a very happy one. He was always happiest at home, and was a tender, loving husband and father. The Browns had three daughters, whom George tended to spoil. Their home was noted for its warm, loving atmosphere.

The Browns supported many worthwhile causes. They were active in helping escaped black American slaves get settled in Canada, in disaster relief to Scotland, in charitable works around Toronto, and in the Temperance Movement. The **Globe** came out in favour of prohibition, as George recognized that alcohol abuse was an enormous problem in Canada.

The Browns also remained faithful to the Presbyterian Free Church throughout their lives. Rarely did they miss church, and George always supported strict Sabbath observance. Throughout his life, the Bible remained George's guide, as he always held it to be God's holy, inspired word, and Jesus to be his Saviour and Lord.

Chapter 9: Reform Reformed

As he took his seat in Parliament at Quebec in August 1852, Brown came as an outsider. He also came with a reputation which had been established because he was the founder, publisher, and editor-in-chief of the **Globe**.

For the Tories of Canada West, he was a sometimes bitter foe who stood against much of what they stood for. For the Hincksite Reformers, he was a former ally who had turned against them because of their failure to fulfil election promises. For the Clear Grits, he was a maverick who had opposed them as radicals in the past, but who now spoke more forcefully than they now did in favour of some of the very things they had aimed for before joining Hincks. For the "Bleus", or Conservatives, of Canada East, he was a radical anti-Catholic, an anti-French *bigot*. For the "Rouges", or Liberals, of Canada East, who were like the Clear Grits in many ways, he was still a bigot, but also an interesting possible ally whom they did not yet know or trust.

In Brown's very first speech soon after Parliament opened, he quickly showed that he was a powerful speaker capable of devastating analysis of his opponents' weaknesses. For over two hours, he held the floor and the full attention of the House. He showed by careful logic and detailed facts that the United Province of Canada's political parties would all have to remake their alliances and policies. They were all grouped in unnatural ways. Hincks's group should join with the Tories and the "Bleus." The Clear Grits should join with the "Rouges." If they didn't, they would end up in chaos, and the voters would be right to believe all of them were liars and mere power-seekers. Although Brown would prove prophetically right, it would be years before they would face up to it.

It did not take too long before the cracks in the Hincks-Clear Grit alliance began to appear. Brown was determined that he would hammer away at the issues he wanted dealt with on every occasion he had. He wanted the Clergy Reserves issue settled; he wanted a stop to the government approving the formation of tax-exempt corporations by religious denominations; he wanted a stop to the expansion of separate Catholic school systems. He began to focus on a new issue as well-that of representation by population, which the **Globe** would dub "Rep. by Pop."

The first three of these questions all had a strong religious side to them. The Roman Catholics did not understand his reasons for insisting so strongly that the government stop mixing politics with religious beliefs. They did not understand Brown's view of Christianity.

"Rep. by Pop." referred to the fact that there were 200,000 to 300,000 more people in Canada West than in Canada East. However, both sections had the same number of MPs. This was obviously not right, said Brown. These 200,000 people effectively had no voice in the country's government. The West should be given more seats. Clearly, there was much potential for serious conflict.

Many of Hincks's uneasy Clear Grit allies felt much as George Brown did, and they resented having to pass laws allowing many special arrangements for Roman Catholic institutions.

By the 1853 session of Parliament, Brown had arrived at what would be the main theme of his Reform program for many years: Representation by Population. As John Lewis explained in his biography of Brown:

> "...Brown's point of view...was this: That the seat of government (Quebec) was a Catholic city, and that legislation and administration were largely controlled by the French-Canadian priesthood. He

complained that Upper Canada was unfairly treated in regard to legislation and expenditure; that its public opinion was disregarded, and that it was not fairly represented. The question of representation steadily assumed more importance in his mind, and he finally came to the conclusion that representation by population was the true remedy for all the grievances of which he complained."(12)

Brown had, within one year of entering Parliament, become the acknowledged voice of the feelings of the majority of Canada West's voters. If he did not have many friends in Parliament, everyone knew he had to be taken very seriously because of his growing influence with the people.

His reputation at the time was summed up by an article about him in the Cobourg **Star**, one of his Tory foes' newspapers:

"In George Brown we see no agitator or demagogue, but the strivings of common sense, a sober will to attain the useful, the practical and the needful. He has patient courage, stubborn endurance, and obstinate resistance, and desperate daring in attacking what he believes to be wrong and in defending what he believes to be right. There is no cant or parade or tinsel or clap-trap about him. He takes his stand against open, palpable, tangible wrongs....He does not slip the word of promise to the ear and then break it to the lips....Change for the sake of change, agitation for vanity, for applause or mischief, he has contemptuously repudiated...."(13)

This was the opinion of even his opponents in Upper Canada. While standing high in public opinion in Canada West, Brown could only work hard and gradually at changing things in Parliament. Three years would go by before it would be possible to once again join the Reformers of Upper Canada into a united political force. For that to happen, these Liberals would have to be ready to bury their differences and recognize the man who was their natural leader – George Brown. It would require those three years for many of the Clear Grits to understand that it had been a dismal mistake to seek power at the price of many compromises. It would require those three years for many Protestants of the West to agree that they had to act together just as the Roman Catholic French-Canadians continued to do.

The lesson of unity was a hard one to learn for free-thinking Protestants like Brown. Brown, so often accused of narrow-minded prejudice in his own time, has been called this even to this day. His opponents' description of him, especially Sir John A. Macdonald's, seems to have carried over into the opinions of modern historians too.

Macdonald seems more like a 21st-Century man with his easy-going, laid-back style and his lack of religious and moral scruples in politics. Brown, for 21st -Century people, is less sympathetic. He had strong principles, would not compromise them, and did not play political games. Brown stood out in this respect then, just as he would now.

Brown was far from perfect, of course. It is forgotten, however, that strong words and language were then common. Politics in the 21st Century seems to be returning to this style. It is forgotten that most people of the 19th century had strong views on religiously related questions and often treated their opponents harshly.

Brown stands out here too in that he said what he meant and meant what he said, whereas many others said harsh things and then compromised to gain power. Therefore, Brown appeared inflexible and prejudiced. It is probably much truer to say that he used strong language because he would not deviate from the truth as he understood it, and he could not abide by blatant dishonesty and lack of integrity in others when he could see it.

In the spring of 1853, Parliament was debating about more support for Catholic schools in Canada West. Brown was insisting that the French-Canadian Catholics of Canada East, controlled by Catholic priests and bishops, had no right to force such laws through against the wishes of the Protestant majority of Upper Canadians.

At this point, Alessandro Gavazzi, an Italian ex-priest turned Protestant, was touring Canada talking about the "evil" plans of the Pope and the Catholic Church. In Canada West he had been very popular. In Quebec City he caused a riot. A mob of Irish Catholics wished to kill him, and almost did. When they could not, they went looking for George Brown, who was in town as a Member of Parliament. Fortunately, they failed to find him.

Regardless of the trouble, Brown continued attacking the proposals for more Catholic schools in Canada West the next day. This just added one more reason for Western Canadians to see Brown as their champion in resisting "French, Catholic power." Amazingly, the Hincks government failed to settle the Clergy Reserves question in either 1853 or 1854, even after the British government finally transferred authority to do so to the Canadian government. This also made Brown appear even more as the man who really represented the wishes of Canada West.

In June 1854 the Hincks government collapsed when the Clear Grits had finally had enough and turned against it. A surprise election was called. In the following campaign, Brown hoped for a strong showing of "voluntaryists", of whatever party. He even supported some Tories who promised to vote to dissolve the Clergy Reserves. He himself was re-elected in a different constituency, Lambton.

In the new Parliament, Brown's main goal was to rebuild the Reform/Liberal Party. Simultaneously, the new government turned out to be an incredible coalition of "moderate" Liberals and old and "new" Conservatives. The new party was an *oxymoron* called the Liberal-Conservative Coalition. The leading members were John A. Macdonald and Georges-Etienne Cartier, although the nominal Prime Minister was Alexander MacNab, the Old Tory leader.

The government started well enough in September 1854. That autumn it disposed of two old issues, the Clergy Reserves of Canada West and the *seigneuries* in Canada East. Even George Brown and the **Globe** were reasonably satisfied with the way the Reserves were finally disposed of. Although he wanted the land sold and the money given to the common, or public schools, Brown accepted that the municipal governments should get it.

Thus one of the most divisive questions of the 19th century was finally brought to a close, and, in most respects, as George Brown had desired. The influence of the **Globe** and of Brown as a politician had no small part in achieving this. Even Macdonald, who actually introduced the law, had recognized that it was inevitable that the Reserves be abolished. For Brown this was a victory for justice and equality of religion.

Meanwhile, the Clear Grits were obviously in need of a leader. The **Globe** and the Grit papers began to talk about this, and that there was no longer any major reason to divide Brown and the Clear Grits. The **Globe** bought the Clear Grit **North American** and its editor, William McDougall, went to work at the **Globe** as Gordon Brown's chief assistant.

In May 1855, just before Parliament was about to end for the summer, and after one half of the Upper Canadian MP's had left for home from far-off Quebec City, Macdonald sneaked in a new law to expand Separate Schools again. Brown protested that this was being done behind the backs of the representatives of the people. The western Protestant majority was again being forced to accept something against their wishes. An eastern French Catholic majority was being used to perform this injustice. This just proved the need for "Rep. by Pop."

Many people of the West felt that the best thing to do would be to separate the two Canadas. Brown opposed this idea vigorously, and so did the **Globe**. Instead, he said, the constitution should be changed to bring in "Rep. by Pop." in East and West, and the country should actually be expanded to take in the Far West. This referred to all the land owned by The Hudson's Bay Company.

Throughout the summer of 1855, the **Globe** promoted Rep. by Pop., and Brown spoke on it constantly. In July, at a special meeting of Reform leaders, Brown won the support of many of them. By September, most of the Grits were ready to support many of Brown's ideas. It seemed that the reforming of the Liberal Party was near. But it did not come for over a year. There was still healing to be done before many Grit supporters could feel comfortable with George Brown.

In the 1856 session of Parliament, it seemed that there was not to be a great deal of controversy. When it came, it was sudden and caught everyone by surprise. Brown had been hammering away at the shakiness of the government coalition under MacNab. The ministers, seeing Brown as their main foe, even though he led no party, made him their special target in their speeches day after day. Led by John A. Macdonald, they accused him of being office hungry.

On the night of February 26, 1856, Brown went on the counterattack after a steady barrage from the ministers. He proceeded to describe in detail how his enemies had acted without principle in setting up the government. They had, he said, done the complete opposite of what they had said they would do in the election in order to be in power. He singled out Macdonald as the main Tory and a government minister.

John A. Macdonald exploded in fury as his case against Brown's "power hunger" was devastatingly refuted. He attacked Brown personally, calling him many vicious names and, finally, resurrecting the old Kingston Penitentiary investigation of 1849. He accused Brown of falsifying and destroying evidence, and bribing witnesses against his friend, ex-Warden Henry Smith! If this were proven, Brown could go to prison. Macdonald said he could prove it.

Brown barely kept control of his temper. The next day he moved that a special committee of inquiry into the penitentiary investigation be set up. He used the words of one of Macdonald's very own motions from a previous parliament. When Macdonald disputed the motion, Brown pointed out that he was fighting his own words and idea. He insisted that the committee be set up at once and conduct an immediate investigation to either prove Macdonald's charges or his own innocence.

It seemed clear as the committee did its work over the next weeks that the government's aim was to discredit Brown and perhaps force him to resign, or at least destroy his credibility. Macdonald packed the committee of seven with five pro-government members and only two opposition members.

Macdonald and his lawyer had assumed that all the original evidence had been destroyed in the burning of the Montreal Parliament buildings.

They intended to show, by calling witnesses, that what witnesses had said and what Brown had reported as secretary of the investigation were different. Alexander Mackenzie, Brown's close friend, wrote of this episode in 1882 as follows:

> "It is said that at one of the first meetings of the committee, Mr. Vankoughnet, counsel for Mr. Macdonald, in moving for an order to examine certain convicts in the penitentiary, stated that unfortunately it was found that the report of the penitentiary commissioners was destroyed in the Montreal fire. He said he regretted this, as, if that report were extant, he would be able to prove his own case without calling such witnesses as he now proposed to put in the box. Mr. Brown was in the committee room sitting with his overcoat on, waiting for the proceedings to commence, and on hearing Mr. Vankoughnet's speech, he unbuttoned his coat, and drawing from it the original report of the commission, said he was happy to hear that that document was all that was wanted, and throwing it on the table, said, "There it is." Mr. Vankoughnet immediately left the room, and meeting Mr. Macdonald, said to him, "Your case is dished.""(14)

Unfortunately, Macdonald did not withdraw his charges. He still hoped to stain Brown somehow. The biased committee tried its best to help him, but found no grounds to charge Brown with anything. The best they could do was to create some suspicion that Brown had overdone it as the commission's secretary. Brown was effectively completely blameless, although Macdonald never withdrew his charges. The most he admitted was that he regretted saying some things he had said. This incident left bitterness and resentment, and Brown was never able to be personally friendly with Macdonald again.

Meanwhile, more and more Grit members and some others from Canada West were voting in line with George Brown on important issues, such as Catholic separate schools. The opposition now had a comfortable majority in Canada West. The government had to rely almost completely on its "French vote" to keep going.

After Parliament quit for the summer, the **Globe** and Brown took up the idea of Rep. By Pop., but now stressed that Canada should take over the Hudson Bay Company's land in the North-West. They pushed this idea so effectively that they won the support of a large number of influential and ordinary Upper Canadians. It was Canada's right; it was God's will; it was Britain's duty to turn it over to Canada. Businessmen, investors, and farmers all supported the idea. They even dreamed of a continental railway across the Prairies to the Rockies from Lake Superior. All of this was very prophetic, and would one day come to pass. Unfortunately, George Brown would not live to see his whole dream fulfilled.

The final reformation of the Reform/Liberal Party took place on January 8, 1857 at a convention called in Toronto at the invitation of the **Globe**. All the major Liberal leaders attended. They set up a party organization and adopted the **Globe**'s and George Brown's suggested program. It included Rep. by Pop. and the acquisition of the North-West as two of its leading policies.

Brown was now the most powerful politician in Upper Canada. He was largely responsible for the recreation of a Reform Party that was now stronger and more united than ever. His program was its program. His newspaper was its mouthpiece. No one in Canada could ignore George Brown or his ideas.

Chapter 10: From Opposition to Opposition

It was in the autumn of 1857 that Brown's sister, Catherine, was killed. November found him depressed and thinking of quitting politics when the Macdonald government decided to call an election rather than meet Parliament again.

The Reform organization swung into action. George Brown, feeling overwhelmed by his many concerns, as well as the loss of his sister, dutifully agreed to run again. But he wanted a riding with less work to do than Lambton. Having already agreed to run for Oxford, a group of Toronto leaders asked him to run in Toronto. He decided to run in both, not sure that he could win in Toronto, which had always voted Tory in the past.

He spent all his time in Toronto, while assistants looked after Oxford. After a tumultuous and sometimes violent campaign, Brown won both ridings. He resigned in Oxford, which William McDougall then won. Overall, the Reform Party won a good majority in Canada West. However, Macdonald's allies in Canada East, *les Bleus,* won a large majority there. The Liberal-Conservatives still held on to power. The opposition was the Liberals under Brown in the West and *les Rouges* under Dorion in the East.

Macdonald and Cartier led the government. They set out no specific program to resolve the problem of the West being under-represented and dominated by the East. The people of the West had shown in the election that they expected a solution by voting for the Reform Party. The West paid between 2/3 and ¾ of the taxes, and had a 20% larger population. Much of the populace felt that the French Catholic East had abused the constitution, and that the government of Conservatives and *Bleus,* aided by turncoat Liberals, was a corrupt bunch interested only in staying in power.

The Reform Party, on the other hand, held to Representation by Population as the only honest and practical solution. While they could understand a concept such as joining all the colonies of British North America to form one country, they did not think that it was realistic at this point, even though some talked about it.

In the session of Parliament that began on February 25, 1858, the Reform and Rouges members, who had begun discussing cooperating before Parliament opened, attacked the government fiercely. They attacked them for having no plan to fix the division between East and West. The attacked them for putting the country deeper and deeper in debt. They attacked them for being corrupt and under the control of the big railroad companies, especially the Grand Trunk Railroad. The government had five ministers who were connected to this company, including Cartier himself, who was its lawyer. Every year millions of dollars were lent by the government to the Grand Trunk.

Macdonald, Cartier, and their Cabinet were under intense pressure. In desperation, they resorted to personal attacks on Brown's reputation. A certain backbench member, Mr. Powell of Carleton, accused Brown and his father of being defaulters on debts. The idea was that such a man could not be trusted to tell the truth.

Brown had often faced such accusations from newspapers and in meetings. He had never replied publicly, because he felt it would serve no purpose, and the accusers were not important enough to merit a reply. But this time an MP was accusing him publicly in Parliament itself, and he did not doubt that this MP represented the views of at least some of the ministers.

Brown rose to explain the whole story of how his father had mixed public money up with his own, how his friends had loaned him the money to repay it, and how he and his father had struggled to pay off the debt since, even though the friends had never laid any obligation upon them to do so. Part of what he said was:

> "....There are those present who have known my every action since I set foot in this country; they know I have not eaten the bread of idleness, but they did not know the great object of my labour. The one end of my desire for wealth was that I might discharge those debts and redeem my father's honour. Thank God, sir, that my exertions have not been in vain. Thank God, sir, I have long possessed property far more than sufficient for all my desires. But...it is one thing in this country to have property, and another to be able to withdraw a large sum of money from a business in active operation...."(15)

Brown explained that he had not explained the matter before because he had no desire to drag his father's private business into public, even though his own father had long wanted to clear it up himself.

On July 28, even some of their own members from Canada West voted against the government on moving the capital of Canada permanently to Ottawa. The government lost the vote. The opposition followed up with a vote to condemn the government. Although Macdonald and Cartier won the second vote, they could see that they were in trouble and some of their own members were close to going over to Brown.

Macdonald and Cartier decided to lay a trap for Brown and Dorion, the Rouges leader. They decided to resign as the government the next morning. They could say that because Queen Victoria herself had chosen

Ottawa because the Canadians had asked her to settle their argument about which city should be the capital, Brown, the Reformers, and the Rouges had insulted her. In fact, Queen Victoria had not really made the choice herself, but had probably followed the Governor-General's advice. Governor-General Sir Edmund Head had suggested Ottawa as a compromise to stop all the bickering about Montreal vs. Toronto, or Quebec vs. Kingston.

By resigning, Macdonald and Cartier hoped to show up the opposition as being unable to agree enough to form their own government. They did not expect George Brown, considered an anti-Catholic bigot and anti-French politician, to be able to make an arrangement with the mostly Catholic Eastern Liberals under Antoine-Aimé Dorion. If the two still did manage to surprise them and come to agreement, then they could defeat them in Parliament because they still had a majority, even if it was shaky. It would then be up to Head to either allow a new election to be called or to ask the "loyal" Macdonald and Cartier team to come back.

What occurred over the next week became known as the "Double Shuffle." Head asked Brown if he could form a government. Brown said he needed time to talk to his friends. For three days Brown, Dorion, and some others worked hard and talked long.

They came to an agreement. Brown returned to Head to say that he could form a government. Head warned Brown that if he lost a vote in Parliament that he would not guarantee that he would call a new election if Brown asked him to. Further, he later in the day sent the two a long letter spelling out to them what he expected them to do before he would grant them an election.

All of this was most extraordinary. No Governor-General had treated any Prime Minister in this fashion since 1841 when the Union began. It smelled like a trap. What could they do? They could not win in Parliament. Their followers expected them to at least try to govern. It seemed that Head was completely prejudiced against them and wanted them to know it. Again, this was "highly irregular" conduct for a supposedly neutral Governor representing a far-off Queen.

Either way they faced humiliation. If they backed down before trying, their enemies could say, "Didn't we say Brown could never form a government?" Their own followers would be angry, and some of them might turn against them. If they went ahead, their enemies would block them and say that they were disloyal and unfit to govern. They went ahead.

In those days if the government changed in between elections there was a rule that said that the members of the new Cabinet had to resign their seats and get re-elected. Therefore, Brown, Dorion, and seven others had to resign. When Parliament met they could not speak or even be in their seats.

Macdonald and company attacked them mercilessly. They then voted "no confidence" and defeated the government. Brown, now at the mercy of a hostile Governor-General, went to Head to ask for a *dissolution*, and permission to hold a new election. Head said no; one had been held just seven months before; the country's business must go on.

The humiliation was complete. The trap had worked. The West was outraged, although Macdonald and Cartier were exultant. Their enemies would be long in getting over this humiliation and master-stroke of cunning political warfare. They could now return to power, but the rules said they had to take different jobs if being sworn in again in the same session of Parliament. At 11:45PM one day, Head swore them in to different portfolios than they had held before they had resigned. They immediately resigned from these posts. At 12:15AM the next day, 30 minutes later, he swore them in to the same positions as they had before they resigned. These were the jobs they really wanted.

But did they also not have to get re-elected? They claimed they did not, because they had already held those offices previously in the same session. Head let them get away with it. This episode was considered an outrage by many people in Canada West. Even some Tories found it distasteful if not immoral. The **Globe** thundered about the betrayal of the spirit of British government and justice by the Governor himself. They demanded Head's recall by the Queen. All to no avail.

For years afterwards Brown's enemies would throw this humiliation in his face. For Brown, it was indeed a very discouraging time. All his efforts seemed to have amounted to nothing. Exhausted and worn out, he was not his old self for a long time. He even entertained the idea of separating Canada West from the East and setting up an American style government there. He let the **Globe**'s editors write and talk about it for months. The British system did not seem to work in a country as divided as Canada, and when men were so baseless in their power-lust as Macdonald and the likes of him. By June 1859, it seemed to Brown that the British style of responsible government in Canada had proved a failure.

The ties of unity that had begun to bring the eastern and western Liberals together also were falling apart, much as Macdonald and Cartier had foreseen, although Dorion and Brown maintained a close friendship.

Chapter 11: In Search of an Exit

By July 1859, Brown had "hit bottom." He was not a man to stay down for too long. He was an optimist by temperament, and all his life he had been loyal to Britain and its style of government. He began to look again at ways to save the Union and solve the Rep by Pop problem, even if Macdonald's "unscrupulous gang" stayed in power.

A *federation* rather than a direct union of the two Canadas seemed one way. Accused of stealing this idea from the government, he explained that he was serious about it. The government was not, as evidenced in their unrealistic scheme of covering their real desire to leave things as they were by talking about joining all the colonies of British North America into one great federation.

The reason this was unrealistic, as attractive an idea as it was, was that the other colonies were not interested. Not only that, but the British government had already told Cartier and Macdonald that the idea was "premature." The government kept this "grand scheme" up its sleeve to avoid real action in the present.

This pattern of "wait long enough and your problems will either go away or solve themselves" was typical of Macdonald. It would cause a lot of trouble for Canada in future times of crisis after Confederation. Because of this trait, Macdonald actually became known as "Old Tomorrow."

In the autumn of 1859, at a great convention to renew the party, the Reform Party of Canada West adopted federation of the two Canadas as its official policy. It rejected dissolving the union completely. The eastern Liberals agreed. On this basis the two sections of the Liberal Party were again able to work together in Parliament. The idea of a great federation of all British North America was officially rejected for the moment, not because it was a bad idea, but because it would take too long. Canada's problems were too urgent to wait indefinitely.

The year 1860 was a difficult one for George Brown. He was burdened with heavy financial problems in his business ventures because of the continuing depression that had begun in 1857. He had bought expensive new presses for the **Globe** and worried that the newspaper would not increase its circulation to pay for them. His enemies attacked him personally, trying to show that he had used his political power to get money for his lumber business and himself.

Although he proved that he had not done anything shameful or dishonest, this was hard to take. As well, there were members of the Reform Party who were unhappy and kept making trouble. In addition, the federation idea, which Brown pushed with great determination, was rejected in Parliament, although the majority of the Canada West members voted for it.

By January of 1861, Brown was tired, weary, and discouraged. He wrote to one of his Reform Party friends, Oliver Mowat, who would later become Premier of Ontario after Confederation: "My dear Mowat, I need not remind you of my determination to retire from Parliamentary life at the earliest possible moment…" He seemed almost to think that he was now more of an obstacle than a help to see things change. Another of his good friends, Luther Holton of Lower Canada, told him he could not simply leave his followers "without a shepherd."

Meanwhile, the United States was sliding into Civil War. This would be a very terrible war that would last for four years, from April 1861 to May 1865 by the time the last shots were fired. Canadians were appalled by the American disaster. The effects of the war on Canada's future would be profound.

In March, 1861, already feeling discouraged about the state of his country, George fell severely ill, and spent more than two months quietly resting while the U.S. exploded into Civil War. In June, with Brown barely beginning to get out and about, the Conservative government called an election for July.

Brown worked hard in the campaign, and neglected his own riding in Toronto. He was defeated, and so was the Reform Party. In order to defeat them, Macdonald had told his members they could vote for Rep by Pop if they wanted to. This helped the Conservatives win in Upper Canada, but it also allowed many Rouge members to be elected in Lower Canada.

For Brown, this was a much needed break and change. For the next two years he was out of active politics. Of course, he was still much involved behind the scenes, giving guidance and advice to reformers, and publishing the **Globe**. But he was able to do many things he enjoyed.

He became even wealthier by investing in land and oil wells near Sarnia. He improved the **Globe**. But the most important thing that happened was his first trip back to Scotland in 25 years in 1862. Although he was saddened that his mother died while he was away, he met and married Anne Nelson. They seemed made for each other. She was ten years younger, but shared many of the same interests. She was highly educated, spoke several languages, had read widely, and shared many of the same beliefs and values as George.

The George Brown who returned from Europe was a different man. He had met many of Britain's most important men while there. He had seen and learned a great deal about Britain and Canada's relationship to her. He would now be a committed family man, drawing his personal comfort and strength from his wife and children, of whom they would have three. He would enjoy being with them more and more over the years, far more than enduring the hard knocks of politics.

As J.M.S. Careless described:
> "....Past memories of all he disliked in public life combined with his present consciousness of happiness...made him shrink from the thought of losing one moment with Anne for the dubious pleasures of parliamentary existence: the bitter wrangles, the frustrations and disappointments, the long night hours, the loneliness of life in rented rooms at distant Quebec."(16)

It was only in 1863 that Brown reluctantly agreed to re-enter Parliament after much persuasion from other Reform leaders that the country still badly needed his leadership and voice in Parliament. He was elected in a *by-election* for South Oxford and was soon once more the recognized leader of the Reform Party.

The government at this time was under a strange alliance of Sandfield Macdonald (no relation to John A.) and Sicotte from Lower Canada. Many Reformers and Rouges were with them, against Brown's wishes and judgment. They had only a two or three vote majority.

Brown and the **Globe**, as well as non-government Reformers, believed that it was a mistake to be in a government that could not push for Rep by Pop or the federation of Canada and the acquisition of the North-West from the Hudson Bay Company. The Liberals in the government found themselves "holding their noses" while strengthening Separate Schools, just as in the Hincks government.

Furthermore, Sandfield did not believe in federation, but in continuing the Union using what he called the "double-majority" principle. On questions that concerned only Canada West, only Canada West members would vote, and vice-versa for Canada East. Very few members shared this view.

The government was defeated on May 12, and a new election called. This time, the Reform Party won in Upper Canada, and the Bleus in the East. Most of the Reform members were still willing to support Sandfield Macdonald, who had now formed a new government with Dorion from the East.

The Sandfield Macdonald-Dorion government managed to stumble along, clinging to power, for ten months. Brown did not officially support it, and he kept on trying to get the government to act on such measures as acquiring the North-West Territories from the Hudson's Bay Company before the United States could. The government did not even get the temporary capital of Canada moved back to Toronto from Quebec, even though the new official capital of Ottawa would not be ready for three years.

Brown did not openly oppose the government, but he did not join it either, for he continued to admonish the Reformers who had joined Sandfield that they were losing their credibility and achieving nothing of the true Reform program. All through this period, Brown longed to be out of politics, home with his wife and their new-born first child. Only a sense of unfulfilled duty kept him in Parliament.

His status was a strange one. He had become the effective leader of the *Clear Grits*, a faction of the Reform Party he had once opposed as too radical, a group that had even tended towards joining the United States. Gradually, the hard-core of Reformers was turning back to the old leader as they realized that the Sandfield-Dorion government had no real principles and was headed for eventual defeat. At the same time, the Reformers who had never supported the government were also turning to Brown for leadership.

On March 21, 1864, the Sandfield Macdonald-Dorion government resigned, no longer able to maintain a majority in Parliament. Parliament was adjourned, as the leaders of the factions sought some new combination that might form an *administration*. Brown took the chance to return to Toronto, his family, and the **Globe**. At the **Globe** he had to take charge again, as his brother Gordon was seriously ill.

The new government was formed by John A. Macdonald, Brown's old enemy, and Taché of Canada East. Like the previous government, it had a very shaky hold on power, and did not seem likely to survive for long. Parliament reopened on May 3, but Brown did not return till May 11.

Brown sadly resigned himself to living in Quebec while his wife and baby daughter were to go to Scotland for the summer. As the session moved into the usual pattern of political manoeuvring, Brown watched the sides sparring for an advantage. More and more Reform members were returning to him, the "old" leader. They realized, as he had been saying for several years, that the Reform program could not be achieved by joining in a "moderate" alliance.

Brown continued to stand for clear principles, *Grit* principles, as opposed to the simple desire to get and hold power for its own sake. He continued to put forward clear proposals for solving Canada's governmental *impasse*. These included, as they always had, Rep. by Pop. But now he was speaking for Rep by Pop in a *federation* of the two Canadas. The two would again be divided, but not totally. Each part would have its own provincial legislature, or Parliament, to deal with matters that only concerned itself. For matters that concerned both, there would be a *federal* Parliament.

The third principle Brown continued to push to the fore was the acquisition by Canada of the North-West, the great Hudson's Bay Company territory. Brown and the Grits declared that these vast lands should be stripped from the Company. They held this view because the Company, they said, was not interested in promoting settlement and development of these lands. Meanwhile, the Americans were pushing West at a rapid rate even as their Civil War continued into its fourth terrible year. If Britain did not turn the virtually empty North-West prairies over to Canada, the Americans would move into it and then claim it by right of occupancy.

The **Globe** extolled the virtues of the great Western lands. It painted a picture of its vast potential in agriculture and natural resources. Linked to an increasingly prosperous Canada, these almost empty territories would flourish and be filled with millions of loyal British subjects, a true jewel in the British Empire.

In Parliament at Quebec, Brown challenged the Macdonald-Taché government to boldly seek new solutions to Canada's woes. He warned that the United States, nearing the end of its terrible Civil War, was not in a mood to renew the Reciprocity Treaty of 1854. Nor was it feeling friendly to either Britain or her North American colonies.

In the back of Brown's mind a new idea was stirring. More than anything, Brown longed to see an end to the endless, tiresome political wrangling and power games. While John A. Macdonald seemed to love the challenge of outmanoeuvring his opponents and gaining and keeping power, George Brown no longer took pleasure in debate for its own sake. Gaining power no longer held a real attraction to him. He said repeatedly to his close friends and family that if he saw that he could do better work to achieve the goals he believed in, he would gladly do it immediately.

In fact, nothing would have pleased him more than to be able to resign and become George Brown, simple newspaper publisher, again. Nothing would give him more happiness and peace than to be able to retire from the often cruel world of politics and devote himself much more fully to his family and their happiness. He still hoped to be able to get away from Parliament in June to accompany Anne and baby Margaret to Scotland, even though it looked as though Parliament might be headed into a summer session. In addition, there was the possibility of yet another election unless some new, unexpected rearrangement of the parties took place to give Macdonald and Taché a clear, strong majority.

This is when he decided to make an offer that would truly test the sincerity and goodwill of his political enemies. He would stake everything on a calculated, great gamble. He would rather risk his reputation and newly restored leadership of the Grits, and possibly see his political career destroyed and his principles discredited, than continue in the old ways.

Chapter 12: The Great Coalition

By spring 1864, George Brown had mellowed considerably on the French-Canadian question. While he still deplored Canada West's domination by the "French power" bloc from the East, "he was prepared at the least to let the French-speaking community go its own way, to concede the cultural duality of Canada, and, at the most, to see valuable attributes in French-Canadians that made possible a constructive future partnership of peoples."(17)

The **Globe** had softened its tone towards the French-speaking half of the country. Brown and his editors admitted that Lower Canada's customs, laws, religion, and language were quite acceptable inside their own territory. The problem was that Lower Canada's religious leaders used their influence on Lower Canada's politicians to affect things in Upper Canada, where they really had no business interfering. This made all the more reason to give each half of the United Province its own local government to watch over its own internal affairs without influence from outside.

Before the fall of the Sandfield Macdonald-Dorion government Brown had been able to start a debate on setting up a special committee to investigate changes to the *constitution*. The idea was brought back after John A. Macdonald and Taché took office. To Brown's surprise, on May 19, 1864, Parliament agreed to set up the committee with George Brown as chairman!

All the leading members of Parliament, including the two Macdonalds, Georges Etienne Cartier, Dorion, and 15 others were drafted into the committee by Brown. At the committee's first meeting, Brown firmly demonstrated his determination that this committee would work hard and sincerely to seek a solution to Canada's deadlocked government problem. As J.M.S. Careless explains: "Brown began the meeting significantly and typically. He strode to the door [of the committee room], locked it, and pocketed the key. "Now gentlemen," he said emphatically, "you must talk about this matter, as you cannot leave this room without coming to me.""(18)

This committee was extremely important. It met eight times behind closed doors, and with no reporters watching or audience to play to, the politicians were able to talk honestly and openly. The French-Canadians and Grits were actually able to hear one another. With hearing came understanding, if not agreement.

The committee's report came to Parliament on June 14, 1864. The general feeling was that everyone was "in favour of changes in the direction of a federative system, applied either to Canada alone or to the whole British North American provinces…" This was real progress. For the first time the French-Canadians were all willing to give up their control of the central Parliament in return for having a separate legislature for just Lower Canada's concerns.

Out of the twenty committee members, only three were opposed to its proposal: John A. Macdonald, Sandfield Macdonald, and an old Grit hardliner, John Scoble. John A., soon to be the "Father of Confederation", at first had no liking at all for the federation idea. He wanted a union of all the provinces with only one Parliament for all. His French-Canadian allies, led by Cartier, could never agree to that. Such a union would leave them in an even worse position than Upper Canada had been in since 1840. Their members would be swamped by English MPs from all the provinces, and they would have no control of their own local affairs.

Although they were in opposing political parties, Brown and Cartier became friends during these meetings. Their friendship would last for the rest of Cartier's life. Considering Brown's reputation as a "French-basher" and anti-Catholic, this was a remarkable thing. It demonstrated that Brown was not inflexible, nor was he an ignorant, fanatical bigot, as his critics often charged then, and have continued to do since. Unfortunately, this caricature of him has "stuck" in almost all the books that deal with this time in Canadian history. In fact, the accusation of being a proud bigot can be disproved many times. Another important Catholic was also among Brown's political friends, Thomas D'Arcy McGee.

Brown presented his committee's report with mixed feelings. Personally, he was lonely, for Anne and baby Margaret had left for Scotland. He hoped to follow soon, but the same day as he handed in his report, the Macdonald-Taché government was defeated in a *non-confidence* vote. This fourth government defeat in two years seemed like strong proof that the Canadian system was a failure in need of urgent fixing. How could things go on like this?

What good would yet another election do, only to bring back the same people and parties in a slightly changed mixture? In a moment of what seemed to many like a time for deep discouragement and frustration, Brown had a brilliant and daring idea. Was not this a Providential, or God-sent, opportunity to put the new agreement on federation to the test? He decided to make a stunning offer to John A. Macdonald and his ministers.

Through two Conservative *backbench MPs*, Brown offered to cooperate with the defeated government if it would honestly work to make the committee's agreement a reality. It was time, Brown said, to put politics and Party differences aside so that something really meaningful could be done to end the impasse. The good of the country demanded it!

Parliament met briefly on June 15, expecting the government to resign and ask the Governor-General, Lord Monck, for permission to call an election. Such an action is termed a *dissolution*. Instead, Monck had told them to try to rebuild the government by asking for the opposition's help.

The two backbenchers had meanwhile talked to Macdonald. Instead of resigning, Macdonald and Cartier asked for a short delay. For two days, Brown and Macdonald and Cartier negotiated by sending messages back and forth.

Finally, at 1:00PM on the 17th, Macdonald and his Finance Minister, Alexander Galt, visited Brown in his hotel room in Quebec. Macdonald insisted that, in the proposed coalition government, Brown *must* be in the *Cabinet*. Brown refused, saying the public would be too shocked that he would serve in a Macdonald-led government. They agreed not to bring personal matters up for discussion.

Brown insisted that they must agree to Rep by Pop. They insisted he had to accept a general North American Federation. Brown replied that he was quite ready to accept this, but thought it unlikely to be achieved before many years went by. He wanted a guarantee that if they found it could not be done at that moment, they would go ahead with a simple federation of Upper and Lower Canada. This would give Rep by Pop in the central Parliament and the two provincial legislatures. They all agreed to this.

The House was to meet at 3:00PM. They had to go and say something, even though they had not yet reached a final, detailed agreement. In the House rumours were flying. John A., it was said, was going to pull off another coup. He rose to explain that the Governor-General had agreed to grant dissolution, but that he had been talking to "a leading member of the opposition with a view to reconstructing the ministry." Who could it be? Everyone was buzzing. Tension filled the air as even the Members of Parliament looked around this way and that. When Macdonald revealed that it was none other than "the member for South Oxford", there were gasps of utter amazement.

George Brown!? How was it possible? The two men despised each other. All eyes were on Brown, and all ears awaited a denial, or some explanation. Some Reform members mumbled of betrayal. Brown rose to speak, aware that this was the most critical moment of his whole political career and perhaps in the history of the country to that time. He said:

> "When the repeated endeavours year after year to get a strong government formed have resulted in constant failure, and we now stand ranged, Upper and Lower Canada, in such an attitude that no dissolution [election] or dozen of dissolutions is likely to bring about a satisfactory change, I am bound to say that the honourable gentlemen opposite [Macdonald and his ministers] are approaching this question with candour and frankness [openness and honesty] worthy of men occupying their position...and I hope that the honourable members will approach it with but one desire: to consider the interests of both sections of the Province, and to find a settlement of our difficulties."(19)

There was a moment of amazement; then the House and packed galleries exploded in stunned cheers and applause. Members from all sides rushed to shake Brown's hand. For the moment, at least, Brown was a national hero. Even the reluctant opposition press found words of praise.

Negotiations went on to conclude the deal. On June 20 the terms were made public. Macdonald agreed to a federation, even if it only gradually took in the rest of British North America. Brown agreed to join the Cabinet with several other Reform members, even though he held out against his own involvement until Lord Monck himself told him, in a polite letter, that he must if the thing was to work. Brown agreed to the general federation of all the British provinces of North America if it were possible. The new government was pledged to get possession of the vast North West Territories from the Hudson's Bay Company.

This was how "the Great Coalition" that was to make Confederation possible came to be. Its initiator and inspirer was George Brown, acting, as he always had, on the basis of his deep, Biblically-informed convictions and beliefs in what was just and best for his country.

Chapter 13: Father of Confederation

It was one thing for the Canadian government to decide to seek a federation of all the British colonies of North America. It was quite another to make it happen. To the east of Canada were the colonies of New Brunswick, Nova Scotia, Prince Edward Island, and Newfoundland. To the west was the colony of British Columbia. It was separated from Canada by over 3200 km of mountains, prairies, and forest wilderness. There was little population in that vast expanse. The largest group of about 12000 was at the Red River settlement with Fort Gary at its centre.

How would it be possible to interest all these separate provinces and regions to combine to form one country? The idea had not been warmly welcomed by the Maritimes (eastern) colonies in the past. They had been satisfied with the prosperity and status they had. British Columbia was too remote, and the vast lands in between B.C. and Canada still actually belonged to the Hudson Bay Company.

But in 1864 there was an important influence pushing the colonies to move closer together. The American Civil War was nearing its end, and it certainly looked as though the North was going to win. The North, or Union, was angry with Britain, and there was talk of turning their huge, battle-hardened armies north to seize Canada. Britain had shown too much sympathy and given too much help to the South in the North's eyes. Britain, some American politicians said, should be punished. Canada would be an easy target to do that.

This left the British North American colonies feeling nervous. Would Britain defend them? Or would she just let them fall into American hands? Or were the Americans just "talking tough" because they were angry? Britain was worried too. Queen Victoria's government did not want a war with the United States.

There were some powerful politicians in Britain, such as the British Liberal leader, Mr. Gladstone, who wanted to simply cut the colonies adrift to look after themselves. Others believed that Britain still had a duty to defend its colonies in North America. However, it was time the colonies began paying their way and arming themselves, not always hiding behind Britain for protection. Their defence should be a combined effort.

These people included Britain's Prime Minister, Lord Palmerston, who believed that Canada was not doing its fair share. It was in this atmosphere that George Brown and two Reform colleagues joined John A. Macdonald to seek a union of the British North American colonies. Brown's position was President of the Council, a very important job that included arranging what laws the government would need to pass. It would also include going to the Maritimes and Britain to talk about uniting the colonies.

John A. Macdonald's role in Confederation was to put together the government that made it happen, and to keep the process moving to a conclusion once it started. He masterfully managed the people and the conferences that were to follow. However, the original idea was not his, and he did not make the crucial offer to bury old differences.

Confederation was not **just** Brown's idea, but he must get part of the credit because he firmly believed in the federal principle as the solution to Rep by Pop and the terrible quarrelling so common in Canadian politics between Canada East and Canada West. It was his initiative that made what became known as "The Great Coalition" possible.

In the process, the supposedly bigoted Brown became fast friends with Georges Etienne Cartier. The French-Canadian leader risked his own reputation and career to the same degree Brown risked his. Both stood to lose "big time" as leaders of their parties if their members refused to support this "alliance with the devil" on the other side. Both risked being called traitors by the citizens of their two regions who had traditionally supported them because of their strong stands against the other's views. Both thus risked their whole career and reputation.

Brown was even possibly risking the **Globe**. If enough people were unhappy with what he did, they could stop buying his newspaper, which might then stop making money. As J.M.S. Careless tells us:

> "As far as the Province of Canada was concerned-and the dynamic power behind the movement lay in the largest, most troubled British province in America-the original design of Confederation had come from Galt in 1858; its practical execution and final realization would be Macdonald's work preeminently; and the bravest, and utterly essential act of acceptance was Cartier's. Yet, by its very nature, Cartier's act was fundamentally passive. The active force that drove the question of union to the point of decision, opened the way to decision through the constitutional committee, and then made the crucial move that transformed a blank wall of deadlock into vistas of nationhood, was George Brown – in all this, the real initiator of Confederation."[20]

What drove Brown to make this crucial move? What inner power motivated him to "cross the floor" and join his long-time foes? Before that memorable event, now forgotten in our history textbooks, what prompted a hostile government to approve Brown's motion to set up a constitutional reform committee to investigate ways of breaking the perpetual deadlock in Canada's government?

From a purely human perspective, historians often accredit such moves to hidden motives or unstated agendas. Politicians and statesmen are undoubtedly ambitious people who seek to gain power and, once on top, try to stay there. It is difficult to find such motivations behind George Brown's conduct in 1864, for the evidence of his words and deeds do not point in that direction. His public and private statements actually contradict such an interpretation.

When we study important historical events, it is necessary to try to discover why the major actors in the events did what they did. We make decisions based on many reasons, only some of which we may actually be able or wish to explain to others. Historical people were just like us, and so we probably can never completely understand why they did what they did or why events happen as they do.

In 1864, we know that George Brown was tired and frustrated with politics as it was in Canada. We know that he was a hard-working, honest, incorruptible leader with a highly developed sense of justice and equality for all. We know that he had very strong opinions, and expressed himself very forcefully on issues that concerned him in both Parliament and the **Globe**. We know that he was a devout Christian, a caring husband and father, a fighter for good causes like settling fugitive slaves in Canada, ending slavery, stopping alcohol abuse, and helping the poor.

He also believed that Canada was a country with great potential that was both badly and unfairly governed. He saw the French Catholic East as unjustly controlling and stifling the development of the rapidly growing and prospering West. One of the ways this was manifested was in the repeated passing of school laws that gave Catholics a privileged position not enjoyed by any other religious group in Canada West. As far as

Brown and the Reform Party were concerned, this was a violation of the Biblical concept of the separation of Church and State.

From Brown's point of view, the Macdonald-Cartier government's approval of the constitutional committee's operation in the spring of 1864 was an unexpected breakthrough. The fact that he was appointed to be its chairman and given a free hand to recruit whomever he pleased as its members was just as remarkable. The fact that Parliament approved the committee's report without debate was another marvel. The committee's recommendations, made by both Liberals and Conservatives, Catholics and Protestants, Eastern and Western representatives, included the conclusion that only a federation based on Rep by Pop could ultimately solve the Canadian problem and remedy an unjust system.

This was the background to Brown's decision to cross the floor of Parliament to sit alongside John A. and end the deadlock once and for all, or face total ruin if the attempt should fail. Somewhere within Brown's spirit, he knew that the God he believed governs the course of nations and the lives of men had opened a door he had almost given up hope of ever seeing opened. He must seize this once-in-a-lifetime opportunity to do something that could actually change the course of history, or he would fail his God, his country, and his own sense of duty and justice. He was willing to take the risk that it just might cost him his reputation, his political career, and perhaps even his livelihood. He was willing to trust God for the result.

The way things came together in 1864 seemed to a large number of participants and observers at the time to be more than coincidence. George Brown, Leonard Tilley of New Brunswick, and others, saw God's will, or "Providence", in it all. They talked about a sense of being engaged in something far greater than themselves. They sensed being privileged to take part in a unique historical adventure not arranged or moved along by mere human planning. As Brown's Irish Catholic friend from Montreal and fellow MP, Thomas D'Arcy McGee expressed it, they were caught up in "events stronger than advocacy, events stronger than men."

At the new government's urging, Governor-General Monck wrote to the Lieutenant Governors of New Brunswick, Nova Scotia, and Prince Edward Island. The Maritime Provinces had already planned a conference to discuss their own union. It was to begin September 1. Monck asked them to receive a Canadian delegation to observe the conference. All the responses were favourable.

Thomas D'Arcy McGee, Brown's new friend, usually spent his summers in the Maritimes. He decided to convert his holiday into a good-will tour and take along as many Canadian Members of Parliament, businessmen, and newspapermen as would go to "talk up" the union of all the colonies.

Back in Quebec, the new coalition Canadian Cabinet worked hard at preparing its plans for the September conference at Charlottetown. In the midst of this, Brown found time to visit Ottawa to inspect the new Parliament buildings. He found them magnificent, even in their incomplete state, but reported to the government that they would not be ready for at least a year. He missed his little family.

Brown had a sense of history in what he and his Cabinet colleagues were doing. It was Brown who chaired the Cabinet discussions as they drafted their proposals for Charlottetown. He enthusiastically wrote to Anne, "I do believe we will succeed!" And he found it humorous when he looked around the table thinking back to times when several of those seated there had bitterly and furiously attacked and denounced him and all he stood for. He admitted to feeling "a regular chuckle of gratified pride - no higher sentiment..." He told his wife, "I don't believe any of us appreciate in its true importance, the immensity of the work we are engaged in."(21)

The Canadian delegation to Charlottetown left aboard the Canadian government steamer *Queen Victoria* on August 29. The eight delegates included John A. Macdonald, Georges Etienne Cartier, Alexander Galt, George Brown, James McDougall, Thomas D'Arcy McGee, Alexander Campbell, and Hector Langevin. They had two clerks and a shorthand writer as well. The weather was beautiful, and the cruise very pleasant.

In Charlottetown the Canadian delegation impressed everyone. The real work began on September 2, and the Canadians dominated the talks, giving one powerful presentation after another. On the afternoon of Saturday, September 3, with the conference meeting aboard the *Queen Victoria*, Cartier and Brown both spoke very eloquently, and everyone agreed that it was time to found a new nation.

On Monday, following the rest-day of Sunday, Brown took the floor and spent the whole day outlining how the new country's government and courts would work, and what the powers of the federal and provincial governments would be. Tuesday was a day for questions and debating, and the Canadians closed their case to let the Maritimers decide what to do. They concluded that the union should go ahead if the terms were "satisfactory."

The conference moved to Halifax for three days and on September 1 the first public announcement of the union plans was made. Of the ten speeches made on that day, Brown's was described as very powerful, even "masterly." The delegates decided to hold a second conference in Quebec to begin on October 10.

When the Quebec conference began, the **Globe** commented, "While we all rejoice, we cannot but remember that we have arrived at the very crisis of our fate." Unlike the Charlottetown-Halifax Conference, the Quebec Conference was hard work. Day after day, the delegates hammered out the framework of the constitution of a new country. Night after night they attended many parties and events designed to cement their relationships and build friendship.

Brown played a prominent role in all these proceedings. He hoped to finish this work in time to sail to Scotland on October 26 to spend the winter with his wife. Yet he knew that if he could not leave till later, his wife would understand and realize the importance of what was being done.

The conference actually did not end till October 27, when Brown wrote happily to Anne, "All right!!! Conference through at six o'clock this evening - constitution adopted - a most creditable document - a complete reform of all the abuses and injustice we have complained of!! Is it not wonderful? French-Canadianism entirely extinguished!"

In that last remark we read again the old frustrations of seeing English Upper Canada dominated by French Lower Canada for over two decades. We hear again the old slogan, now fulfilled, of "Rep by Pop! Rep by Pop!"

We are not justified in reading our own time's prejudices and political correctness into it. Brown was expressing his happiness that Ontario would no longer be a prisoner to the French-speaking wing of the Roman Catholic Church in Canada. He was not aiming to "extinguish" all French Canadians in Canada, or eliminate all French influence from the newly emerging country of Canada.

Following a speaking tour to promote the proposed new nation, Brown took a fast ship, the *Persia*, to Liverpool, England on November 16. He was accompanied by Colonel Jervois, who had written an important study of Canada's defence which emphasized Britain's continued responsibility while recognizing that Canada should do more for itself too. Brown was to discuss this, as well as the proposed colonial "confederation", with the British government's leaders during his visit.

He first went straight to Edinburgh to be with Anne for their wedding anniversary. When Brown went to London in December, he found the British government very favourable to Confederation. On the defence issue, it became clear that some people in the British government desired that "ere long, the British colonies should shift for themselves." Some British officials, it seemed, wished that Canada would simply declare its independence.

The Browns returned to Canada in January, 1865. By January 19, George was back in Quebec City in order to take part in the Parliamentary debates on Confederation that were due to begin. The opponents of Confederation in Canada were the *Rouges* under Brown's old friend Dorion, and a rump of disgruntled Canada West Reformers led by Sandfield Macdonald.

Brown's speech in the debate took the whole evening of February 8, 1865. He had worked long and hard on it. Once again he invoked the sense of history:

> "The scene presented by this chamber at this moment, I venture to affirm has few parallels in history. One hundred years has passed away since these provinces became by conquest part of the British Empire. I speak in no boastful spirit-I desire not for a moment to excite a painful thought what was then the fortune of war might have been ours on that well-fought field. I recall those olden times

> merely to mark the fact that here sit today the descendants of the victors and the vanquished in the fight of 1759, with all the differences of language, religion, civil law and social habit nearly as distinctly marked as they were a century ago. Here we sit today seeking amicably to find a remedy for constitutional evils and injustice complained of - by the vanquished? No, but complained of by the conquerors! Here sit the representatives of the British population claiming justice - only justice; and here sit the representatives of the French population discussing in the French tongue whether we shall have it. One hundred years have passed away since the conquest of Quebec, but here sit the children of victor and vanquished, all avowing hearty attachment to the British crown, all earnestly deliberating how we shall best extend the blessing of British institutions- how a great people may be established on this continent in close connection with Great Britain. Where in the pages of history shall we find a parallel to this?"(22)

Brown's conviction about the "hand of Providence" being seen at work in the achievement of the proposed new country uniting the provinces of British North America was echoed by one of his new friends, Thomas D'Arcy McGee of Montreal. McGee spoke in Parliament on February 9, 1865, the day after Brown. Here is part of what he said in urging the Canadian Parliament to ratify the resolutions of the Quebec Conference of October 1864:

> "The strange and fortunate events that have occurred in Canada, the extraordinary concessions made by the leaders of the governments below—Dr. Tupper, the Nova Scotia premier, for instance...can we ever expect, if we reject this scheme, that the same or similar things will occur again to favour it? Can we expect to see the leader of the Upper Canadian Conservative Party and the leader of the Upper Canadian Liberals sitting side by side again, if this project fails to work out, in a spirit of mutual compromise and concession, the problem of our constitutional difficulties? No, sir, it is too much to expect.

"Miracles would cease to be miracles if they were events of everyday occurrence; the very nature of wonders requires that they should be rare; and this is a miraculous and wonderful circumstance...." (23)

But the opposition in Canada was nothing compared to the difficulties the plan soon ran into in the other provinces. In Newfoundland, which had sent delegates to Quebec, the people petitioned for an election before they would commit themselves. The Legislature of Prince Edward Island voted the plan down by 23 to 5 in late March. In New Brunswick, the Lieutenant Governor interfered and pressured Leonard Tilley, the Premier, to call an election.

In Nova Scotia, Joseph Howe, an influential journalist and politician who was upset because he had missed the two big conferences because of other duties, organized strong opposition. He said what many were thinking-that Confederation was a good scheme for Canada – but not for the Maritimes, who would become mere appendages of the middle of the new country.

In New Brunswick the March 1865 election was a disaster for Confederation. Tilley and his whole Cabinet were defeated. The Canadian Parliament passed the 72 Quebec Resolutions anyway on March 11. The Canadian government was determined to go ahead and named Macdonald, Cartier, Galt, and Brown to go to England to officially present the plan to the British Government. There were no Maritime representatives at all, not even from Nova Scotia where Charles Tupper, the pro-Confederation premier, was still holding on to power. But Tupper had been forced to put the project on hold as "impracticable" for the present.

The Canadian trip to Britain was, on the whole, a great success. The British government pledged its support for Confederation. The Canadian statesmen were treated with lavish hospitality. The only problem was defence. The British seemed very reluctant to commit themselves to any real help for Canada if the United States attacked it, as many were afraid they would now that the Civil War had recently ended. Brown, however, never believed the Americans would attack, although he recognized that Canada's defences needed strengthening.

Back in Canada, after they had returned in June, the American threat had diminished, but a group of Irish Americans, many of whom had fought for the North in the Civil War, had decided to conquer Canada anyway, even without the U.S. government's help. These men, called the Fenians, thought that by conquering Canada, they could hold it hostage till Britain agreed to give Ireland its independence.

This scheme was crazy, but the American government allowed the Fenians to drill and gather near the Canadian and New Brunswick borders. This, and pressure by Britain stating the Mother Country's approval of the Confederation plan, caused the Maritimers to begin to reconsider.

In August 1865, George Brown almost resigned from the Great Coalition. The nominal Prime Minister, Taché, died suddenly. Governor-General Monck, needing a new Prime Minister, offered the post to John A. Macdonald as the most senior minister of the government. Brown did not want the job himself, but, he informed Monck, he could not serve under Macdonald as his subordinate.

There was probably a mixture of reasons for this. The old wounds between them were not healed, even after working together for over a year. Macdonald in charge would make it look as though the government was now a Conservative government, and Brown would look as though he had abandoned his Liberal members of Parliament and friends. No, said Brown, if he were to continue, there must be a neutral figure-head Prime Minister like Taché as Prime Minister.

Macdonald had a hard time accepting this, but he did for the sake of the Confederation project. The new Prime Minister was Sir Narcisse Belleau, a minor Legislative Council member. The real leader was, as everyone knew, John A. Macdonald. Brown continued, with increasing discomfort, in the Cabinet. In November 1865, he was sent on a solo mission to New Brunswick and Nova Scotia to see if Confederation could be restarted there.

He found things looking hopeful in New Brunswick. Lieutenant-Governor Gordon had been told by London to support Confederation. A well-known confederationist had just been re-elected in the Legislature in a by-election. The Confederalists thought they might regain power in 1866. In Nova Scotia, Tupper still thought he must wait until New Brunswick made up its mind before he could try to push Confederation through his Legislature.

When Brown returned to Quebec in December 1865, he found out that Galt, the Canadian Finance Minister, had, he believed, improperly negotiated with the Americans about trade arrangements behind the backs of the other partners in Confederation. Galt's action must be reprimanded, and the other provinces brought into any negotiations, he insisted. His views were firmly refused by all the conservative Cabinet ministers.

Brown felt the time had come for him to quit the government. He felt his work for Confederation was done. All the ground work was complete, and the others could finish it up just as well without him. He did not wish to find himself in a Cabinet that was beginning to go back to behaving along straight party lines. He would end up having to support decisions he felt were wrong, just to be there when Confederation matters were discussed.

On December 19, 1865, George Brown resigned from the government. He telegraphed his wife, "Thank Providence - I am a free man once more." As for his relationship with Macdonald, it returned to its old condition of silence.

Chapter 14: Life after Politics

The **Globe of** July 1, 1867 rejoiced in the birth of the new Dominion of Canada. The **Globe**'s publisher had sat up all night writing the lead article which, in more than 9000 words, outlined the infant country's history, birth, and resources. Brown described the new nation's future in glowing terms.

In Ottawa, Brown's old Great Coalition Cabinet partners had all just been knighted. John A. Macdonald was now *Sir* John A. Macdonald. But Brown was not there and not knighted. Governor-General Monck wrote to him apologetically: "...I was mortified and disappointed that circumstances had rendered it impossible for me to recommend for a share in those distinctions *the* man whose conduct in 1864 had rendered the project of union feasible ." There is no doubt that Brown was hurt by this exclusion, for he had risked far more than any of the others, except Cartier, at the time.

Between December 1865 and July 1867, Brown had concentrated on his family and personal business. At the end of June 1867, there had been a great convention to rebuild the Liberal Party in Ontario for the time after Confederation took effect. Brown had played an important part in it, convincing delegates that the time for coalition was over. He warned those that wanted to continue working with Sir John A. that they would end up being Tories supporting the Conservative program.

Many Liberals wanted Brown to return to Parliament. He did not want to, but ran for the constituency of Whitby in August, and lost to the Conservative. The residents saw him as an outsider, while the conservative, Mr. Gibbs, was a well-known local man. The Liberals did not do well at all in the first election after Confederation. The

Conservatives swept the country. The Liberals would have to start almost from scratch in every province.

Brown felt that his usefulness as a Leader of the Liberal Party was over. Someone else should take up the job. He could be most helpful by concentrating on keeping the **Globe** the most respected and influential newspaper in Canada. It was some consolation to Brown to see that by 1869, the Reform members of Macdonald's "no-partisanship patriotic coalition" Cabinet were both out of office. This, Brown claimed, proved for all to see that the whole thing had only been a disguise for Macdonald and the Conservatives to get a firm hold on power in the new national Parliament in Ottawa.

Brown retired as leader in September 1867. He was content that he had, after all, achieved what he had set out to do when he had first entered politics in 1851. The country had Rep by Pop. Ontario and Quebec each had their own governments to look after their own affairs without interference from the other. The eastern and central colonies of British North America had been united into one strong country under Britain's protection.

Macdonald went on to become a great Prime Minister, Canada's first, serving from 1867 to 1873, and then from 1878 to 1891, when he died. He has become, for many Canadians, historians included, an almost legendary hero who almost single-handedly built the country. His old, fiery-tongued opponent, George Brown, has rarely been appreciated or understood since that time, and has suffered in comparison to the charismatic political master that Macdonald was.

Contrary to the public image of Brown, we find that at home and with his friends he was very different. He loved to be with his wife and children, and was fun-loving. He enjoyed romping with the children, who were always delighted when their father came home. In private life, he immensely enjoyed joking and the company of good friends.

In writing or speaking about political questions, he did not spare his enemies from very strong attacks. That was the style of the time. Brown made it a point of honour never to publicly write or say anything that he felt he could not back up with hard evidence. We live in a far different time with our access to endless news and information, both real and fake, actual and invented. We would do well to follow Brown's scrupulous example in ensuring that the truth and accuracy of whatever the **Globe** published could be independently verified.

Although he was sued more than once for libel, he and the **Globe** were never found guilty of it. Contrary to Brown's sometimes deserved reputation for being anti-French and anti-Catholic, in 1871 he went out of his way to welcome Catholics into the Ontario Liberal Party. In fact, Catholics in the party had never been blocked from leadership or influence. In the Conservative Party in Ontario, however, Catholics seemed unable to gain any influence for a long time, and almost never could get elected.

While Georges-Etienne Cartier always remained a staunch Catholic, he had developed a warm regard and high respect for George Brown from 1964 on. Their personal religious convictions had no bearing on their friendship. Brown reciprocated Cartier's respect, as Cartier had shared the crucial role of risking everything to make Confederation happen. After Brown retired in September 1867, Cartier and Brown wrote one another regularly. Cartier longed for Brown to return to Parliament, and hinted that he would be tempted to join him and leave Macdonald if he returned.

As an employer Brown had a reputation of being strict but fair. He paid his employees well, for the time. He was sympathetic to their personal needs. Like almost all employers of the mid-nineteenth century, he did not like unions. He strongly believed they had a right to exist as a kind of club, but had no right to interfere in the running of a business which they did not own.

His beliefs in this area were not just a kind of upper-class prejudice against working people, as in the case of many other businessmen. Brown firmly believed that society was meant to function socially, politically, and economically according to a set of rules that were rooted in the way God had intended things to work. The principles for these rules were found in the Bible, which he believed was the inspired Word of God. As the historian J.M.S. Careless wrote, "...his attitude...reflected an intellectually consistent set of doctrines regarding economic freedom and natural laws that he ardently believed were right and almost divinely revealed."(23)

This explains Brown's actions during a strike by the printers of the **Globe** and other Toronto newspapers in 1872. Brown has been greatly criticized by some historians over this episode because of his inflexibility, and yet even the printers admitted that Brown was the fairest employer of all those the printers acted against.

In 1870, Manitoba became a province after Louis Riel led the Métis in a rebellion against the Canadian took over the West without consulting them about their needs. British Columbia joined Canada in 1871 after Cartier promised that Canada would build a railway across the Prairies to link it to the rest of the country within ten years. In 1873, Prince Edward Island reversed its decision and decided to join Canada, eight years after the Quebec Conference of 1864.

In late 1873, Brown's old friend and loyal supporter, Alexander Mackenzie, became the first Liberal Prime Minister of Canada. Sir John A. Macdonald's government, re-elected in 1872, had been caught taking $350,000 to finance their election campaign in 1872 from Sir Hugh Allan, a Montreal industrialist who wanted the right to build the Canadian Pacific Railway to B.C. Forced to resign over the scandal, the Macdonald government went down in disgrace, and the Liberals, led by Mackenzie, won a majority.

Mackenzie wanted to recognize and honour his old friend, who had been snubbed at the time of Confederation when all the "Sirs" were handed out to everyone but him. He named Brown to the Canadian Senate, and Brown accepted. Brown returned to Parliament without all the pressures of elections or heavy worries of Cabinet office.

In 1875, Sir Oliver Mowat, who had become Premier of Ontario, nominated his old leader, George Brown, as Lieutenant-Governor of his province. Brown, believing himself unworthy of such an honour, and thinking he could contribute more to Canada from the Senate in Ottawa, turned down the nomination.

A subject that had long grieved Brown's heart was the more than thirty year old division of Canada's Presbyterians into quarrelling factions. In the 1870s, a movement was put on foot to reunite the Presbyterians of Canada by founding a new church in the Presbyterian family which would leave behind the differences carried over from the "Old Sod" of Scotland. These differences were no longer relevant in the New World, where freedom and democracy were uniting people from many backgrounds. In each province, a board of sponsors for the new Presbyterian Church of Canada was recruited to promote and establish the church. Brown was very happy to serve on the board for Ontario, and rejoiced when the new church was officially inaugurated in 1875. Surely the healing of old wounds was pleasing to the Lord!

From 1875 on Brown played less and less a role in political affairs, and became more and more a private man, devoted to his family, his charitable work, his church, and business. The **Globe** continued to prosper with George as the Publisher and Business Manager and Gordon as the General Manager and Editor-in-Chief. Occasionally George would take a direct hand in writing, and sometimes he and Gordon had strong and loud disagreements over editorial policy. But they always resolved these, and would get along well afterwards.

Chapter 15: The Final Act

In May 1879, twelve years after Confederation, Senator George Brown's distinguished contributions to the making of Canada were finally recognized with the offer of a knighthood. He would be able to sign his name *Sir* George Brown, like Sir John A. Macdonald. Brown once again declined a great public honour. By this time in his life, being a knight seemed to have lost its shine to Brown. Everybody and anybody seemed to have been knighted, even when they had contributed only insignificantly to building the country.

On December 2, 1879, disaster struck Brown's already struggling model stockbreeding farm in southern Ontario. Seven of the ten main buildings burned to the ground. Huge amounts of equipment, feed, and hay were lost, along with most of the work horses, pigs, and sheep. Only the cattle were saved from the wreckage. The losses in money were enormous.

On Christmas Day, 1879, the final straw came. The temporary stable rigged since the disaster also burned down. More horses were lost, and all the feed and other equipment assembled since the first fire as well.

Brown, at home in Toronto when he got the news, broke down and wept. He never went back to his farm again.

On March 25, 1880, at 4:30PM, a small, unhealthy looking man knocked on Publisher Brown's office door. Brown did not know him. He was George Bennett, a former employee of the **Globe**. He wanted Mr. Brown to sign a paper stating that he had been employed for five years in the printing shop.

Brown was irritated at being interrupted. He told Bennett to go see his old foreman to get such a certificate. Bennett got upset; the foreman had already refused to sign it. "Then take it to the Treasurer," Brown suggested. No; he wanted Mr. Brown to sign – *now*!

Brown began to lose his temper. He rose from his desk, and firmly told Bennett he would not sign the paper, and to leave his office. Bennett, shouting, ordered Brown to sign. Brown, who towered over Bennett, just as loudly refused. Bennett was white, and his eyes stared unblinking.

He pulled out a revolver and cocked it. Brown leaped and grabbed Bennett's wrist, deflecting the gun down. It fired, and the bullet superficially wounded Brown's thigh. Brown shouted, "Help! Help! Murder!" He still managed to pin Bennett to the wall and wrench the gun away from him.

Help arrived. The police and a doctor were sent for. The wound was not serious. The doctor dressed the wound and told Brown to go home to bed for a few days. Brown walked down the stairs and took a cab home as he usually did. At home he went to bed, as he'd been told to do. Many people sent messages of shock and sympathy. Everyone thought the injury was slight and would not put Brown out of commission for long. He had always been a robust, healthy man.

After four days in bed the wound was not getting better, but worse. It was infected, and these were the days before antiseptics and antibiotics. Brown did not take well to being confined to the house. He was worried about the **Globe**, which he had once more expanded and modernized, but which therefore needed more circulation. His heart was still broken over the destruction of his beloved Bow Park farm.

Brown's condition seemed to improve around mid-April, but a week later, the wound was seen to have gangrene in it. The doctors could not stop the march of the infection. His family and friends still hoped, and many came to visit. He began to lapse into periods of unconsciousness.

When he was awake, he seemed saddened by a sense of failure. He was not leaving his dear Anne and the children with the secure future he had striven to assure. He knew he was dying.

To his sister, Marianne, he said one day, "I have tried to do my duty in the sight of God. I've worked hard for my country, my family and myself. But I have failed. I haven't accomplished what I would have liked."

She replied, "We all fail, and God knows if we were seeking to do our duty when we fail." This comforted him.

He never complained about his physical suffering. Not one word about his pain came from him. In the last few days of his life, he slipped in and out of a coma. He could no longer speak. He still recognized his loved ones when he was conscious, and looked at them with tender, loving eyes.

Early Sunday morning, May 9, 1880, as day was breaking and church bells were sounding Matins, George Brown's spirit returned to God who had given it.

Epilogue

George Brown's sense of failure in his last few days on earth was not the judgment of his family, friends, or country. The tributes to him poured in from everyone who had known him, even his political foes. All recognized his honesty, integrity, and strong sense of duty and conviction. All recognized his great contributions to the making of Canada.

Those who knew him more personally and shared his faith had no doubt as to where he had gone when he left his earthly home. The testimonies of his Christian character and example in many areas were plentiful. His Pastor testified that on his deathbed he had reaffirmed that all his hopes and trust were in his Lord and Saviour, Jesus Christ, and that death itself held no terror for him. He only regretted leaving those he loved so much in such an untimely way.

What were the foundations of Brown's faith? He was born into a Bible-believing, God-fearing, and Christ-honouring home. He was brought up in a home where the Bible was read as a family, and Christian character was exemplified. Theology and learning were not contradictory but complementary. Young George sat in on many discussions about theology, religion, politics, justice, missions, and business with the visitors his father frequently invited home. Godliness was expected, and church-life was an extension of the home. There was ample involvement in good works in the community, and active Christian life included working for justice and righteousness in public life as well as personally practising it in private.

Like all of us, George Brown was far from a perfect man, but Brown's character and witness as a Christian statesman, church member, husband and father, and business leader shone brightly to his family, friends, co-workers, and opponents. It is only just to recognize that Brown was such a man due to his having been a committed, convinced Christian until his dying breath.

Would Canada have become a nation without George Brown's courageous action in 1864? That is one of those questions at which we can only guess. The will to bring the feuding parties together did not seem to exist. The person with the courage to initiate change at great personal risk did not seem to be there. The historical record says clearly that it was one man alone who actually rose above the quarrels, animosities, and rivalries, even against his own personal dislike of the other leader with whom he had to work, to take that risk.

We do not diminish the contributions of Macdonald, Cartier, or Galt in putting forward those of George Brown. It is not an insult to the ability and political wisdom of Sir John A. Macdonald to recognize that he did not inspire Confederation. That honour must justly go to a man whom he always, till his own death in 1891, recognized as having been his most implacable and greatest opponent, George Brown.

Brown's public and private lives were, on the whole, of a piece – that is to say, he lived by a consistent set of Christian convictions and principles at home, in business, and in politics. Not all Christians then agreed with him, nor would they now. But that he was a Christian man seeking to do his Christian duty as a citizen, journalist, husband, and father, there can be no doubt.

The legacy he left behind continues today in many ways. The Reform Party of Upper Canada which he led and inspired for so long became the backbone of the Liberal Party of Canada, the party of Prime Ministers Sir Alexander Mackenzie, Sir Wilfrid Laurier, William Lyon Mackenzie King, Louis St. Laurent, Lester B. Pearson, Pierre Elliott Trudeau, John Turner, Jean Chrétien, Paul Martin and, as of the time of this revision, Justin Trudeau. The Toronto **Globe** is now "Canada's National Newspaper," the **Globe and Mail**.

The Liberal Party and the world of Canadian journalism are thus two major areas where his influence is still seen in Canada to this day, even though he would doubtless be personally outraged by some of the things these two national Canadian institutions have done and stood for over the last 140 years or so.

Let us end with the motto he adopted for the **Globe**, and which appeared for many years as the heading of its front page and that of its successor. It reminds us of his own belief that God has given everyone the right, the freedom, and the duty to act according to his conscience under God. No government has the right to tell anyone what they should believe, or to impose a religious view on its citizens. Neither should governments force subjects to go against God's laws.

Here is his motto: *"The subject who is truly loyal to the chief magistrate will neither advise nor submit to arbitrary measures."*

Endnotes

(1) J.M.S. Careless, **Brown of the Globe, v.1**, (Toronto: Macmillan Company of Canada, 1959) p.6.

(2) Careless, **Brown of the Globe**, v.1, p.8.

(3) Careless, **Brown of the Globe**, v.1, p.22.

(4) Careless, **Brown of the Globe**, v.1, p.22.

(5) John Lewis, **George Brown, The Makers of Canada**, (Toronto: Morang & Co., Limited, 1906) p.7.

(6) Alexander Mackenzie, **The Life and Speeches of Hon. George Brown**, (Toronto: Globe Printing Company, 1882) p.23.

(7) Careless, **Brown of the Globe, v.1**, p.120.

(8) Careless, **v.1**, p.122.

(9) Mackenzie, **Life and Speeches**, p.125.

(10) John Lewis, **George Brown,** (Toronto: Morang & Co. Ltd., 1906) p. 56.

(11) Lewis, **George Brown**, pp.70-71.

(12) Lewis, pp.72-73.

(13) Mackenzie, **Life and Speeches,** p.57.

(14) Lewis, p.95.

(15) Careless, **v.2**, p83.

(16) Careless, **v.2**, p.109.

(17) Careless, **v.2**, p.127.

(18) Careless, **v.2**, p.134.

(19) Careless, **v.2**, p.146.

(20) As reported in Careless, **v.2**, pp.150-151.

(21) Quoted in Careless, **v.2**, pp.182-183.

(22) Careless, **v.2**, p.290.

(23) Ajzenstat, Janet, et al. (eds.). **Canada's Founding Debates**. (Toronto: Stoddart, 1999. © William D. Gairdner) p. 429

APPENDIX: Government and Politics in Canada 1840-67

In 1840, the two colonies or provinces of the British Empire called Upper Canada, now called Ontario, and Lower Canada, now called Quebec, were joined as a single colony, **The United Province of Canada**. There was only one Legislature or Parliament for the two sections, but each section has its own *political parties*.

The two political parties in Canada West in the 1840s were usually called the *Tories* and the *Reform*. They were also known as the Conservatives and the Liberals respectively. In some ways these two parties were like the Conservatives and Liberals of modern Canada, although there were many differences as well.

There were also two political parties in Canada East at the time. They were the *Bleus* and the *Rouges*. The Bleus were conservative, something like the Tories of Canada West. Therefore, the Tories and the Bleus often worked together to form governments. The Bleus wanted to maintain strong links to the Catholic Church in Canada East, just as the Tories in Canada West supported the claims of the Anglican Church to special status. In the early and mid-1840s, both these parties, the Tories and Bleus, preferred to depend on their links to the Governor-General to get power.

The Rouges of Canada East were something like the Reform Party of Canada West. They did not however, seek to combine with the Reform Party at first. Their working together would only come years later. The Rouges were against the power of the Roman Catholic Church in politics, and wanted the government to be more **democratic**.

The following diagram illustrates the political parties of each half of the Province of Canada during the period 1840-67.

1840-1867

Canada West (Upper Canada)   **Canada East (Lower Canada)**
(Ontario after 1867)   **(Quebec (after 1867)**
    Tories   (Conservatives)   Bleus
    Reform   (Liberals)   Rouges

The name "Canada" at that time applied to only Canada East, which is Quebec today, and Canada West, or today's Ontario. Newfoundland, Prince Edward Island, Nova Scotia, and New Brunswick were separate colonies, or provinces, with their own Lieutenant-Governors. The Governor-General of British North America, as people then called all the land controlled by Britain in North America, was also the Governor of the United Province of Canada.

Canada East and Canada West had been united in 1840 after Governor-General John Lambton, Lord Durham, had recommended this in his famous report (see Introduction). Before 1840, Canada West was called Upper Canada and Canada East was known as Lower Canada. The two were separate colonies with their own Governors. After the union of 1840, they were the United Province of Canada, until 1867. At Confederation, they were again separated as the Provinces of Ontario and Quebec.

After 1840, people still often called the two areas Upper and Lower Canada, and even today Ontarians sometimes call their province Upper Canada. Lord Durham said uniting the two colonies was necessary as a result of the rebellions which had occurred in Upper Canada in 1837, and in Lower Canada in 1837-8.

Uniting the two would make British administration and control easier. It would also, he thought, allow the English-speaking people of the West to combine with the English minority of Canada East to dominate, and control, the French-Canadians. Durham hoped the French would gradually lose their culture and learn English if enough English-speaking people came to Canada. To make sure the English did gain dominance and political control, he recommended that the British colonies of North America also be granted **Responsible Government**. This would also ensure that rebellions would not recur.

Responsible Government involves a number of things. It is a form of democracy that operates by having the voters choose representatives to speak for them in a **Parliament**, or **Legislature**. The political party that has the most representatives elected "forms the government." The government must be able to get laws passed in the Legislature; therefore it needs a **majority** in the Legislature.

The leader of the governing party becomes the Prime Minister when (s)he is asked by the **Governor-General** to form a government. To do this, (s)he selects some of his/her members who are representatives in the Legislature, or "have seats", to become **ministers**. The Ministers together are **"the Cabinet"**. A minister is **responsible** for a **Ministry, Department,** or **Portfolio**. (Sh/H)e is in charge of that section of the government, to see that the laws concerning it are carried out, to administer the expenses of the department, and to bring in new laws when needed concerning the government business (s)he is concerned with. (Sh/H)e is responsible to answer to Parliament for how (s)he and the people of his/her department do their jobs and how money is spent by his/her department.

The idea of **Responsible Government** can be illustrated as follows in **Figure 2.** According to Durham's recommendation, the British government had granted Canada responsible government. In other words, adult men with a certain amount of property were given the right to vote for members of the legislature. The Governor-General was supposed to ask the political party leader who had the most supporters in the legislature to be in charge. But, after initially trying it from 1841-44, the people of Canada elected a Tory government that was opposed to this new system. In addition, the Governor General, Lord Metcalfe, had been strongly against it and had even dismissed the Reform ministers and ruled alone for many months before the election.

Many Reformers thus felt that the system had been designed to fail while looking as if it was democratic. However, they were loyal British subjects, and were determined to work to change the system from within by winning elections, even if that were to prove very difficult.

Figure 2 – Parliamentary Responsible Government

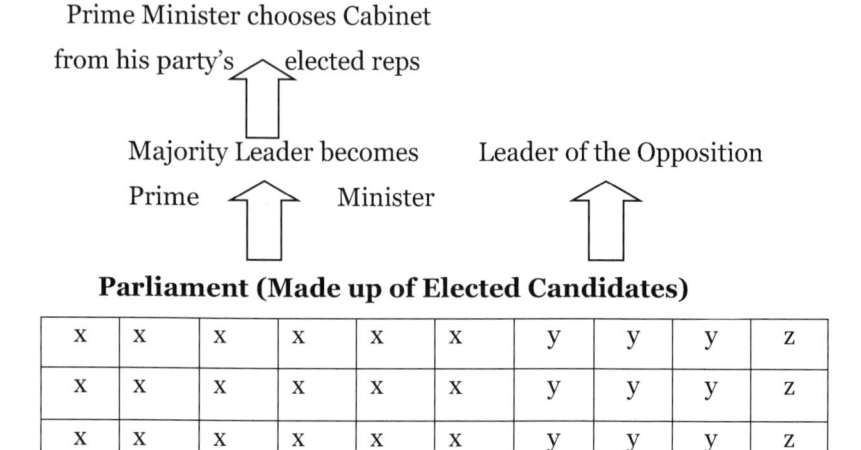

Government   **Opposition**

Prime Minister chooses Cabinet from his party's elected reps

⬆

Majority Leader becomes Prime Minister   Leader of the Opposition

⬆   ⬆

Parliament (Made up of Elected Candidates)

x	x	x	x	x	x	y	y	y	z
x	x	x	x	x	x	y	y	y	z
x	x	x	x	x	x	y	y	y	z
x	x	x	x	x	x	y	y	y	z

MAJORITY PARTY   **OTHER PARTIES**
(Forms Government)   **(Opposition)**

Election (choose your local MP from among the Candidates)

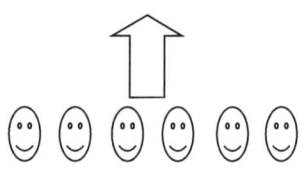

⬆

😊 😊 😊 😊 😊 😊

Electorate – Citizens with the right to vote

Photos and Illustrations

George Brown ca 1864
Library and Archives, Canada

Georges-Etienne Cartier, ca 1864
Patrimoine culturel du Québec

John A. Macdonald, ca 1864
Library and Archives, Canada

Toronto Globe Building ca 1864
Library and Archives Canada

Charlottetown Conference of 1864

Delegates to Charlottetown Conference,
Sept. 18, 1864
Library and Archives Canada

The delegates to the Quebec Conference

Delegates to Quebec Conference, Oct. 1864
Library and Archives Canada

The attack on George Brown, 1882
The Torontoist

Short Select Bibliography

Primary Sources:

Ajzenstat, Janet, et al. (eds.). **Canada's Founding Debates.** © William D. Gairdner. Toronto: Stoddart, 1999..

The Globe, 1843-1880.

Mackenzie, Sir Alexander. **The Life and Speeches of the Honourable George Brown.** Toronto: Globe Printing, 1882.

Pope, Sir Joseph. **Memoirs of the Right Honourable Sir John Alexander Macdonald, G.C.B., First Prime Minister of the Dominion of Canada.** Toronto: 1894.

Secondary Sources:

Biggar, C.R.W. **Sir Oliver Mowat, a Biographical Sketch.** Toronto: Warwick Brothers and Rutter, Limited, 1905.

Brady, Alexander. **Thomas D'Arcy McGee.** Toronto: The Macmillan Company of Canada Limited, 1925.

Careless, J.M.S. **Brown of the Globe. 2 vols.** Toronto: Macmillan, 1959, 1963. (contains many citations of primary sources)

Creighton, Donald. **John A. Macdonald, Vol. 1. The Young Politician.** Toronto: Macmillan, 1952.

Colquhoun, A.H.U. **The Fathers of Confederation. The Chronicles of Canada, 28.** Toronto: Glasgow, Brook and Company, 1916. (Also contains primary source citations)

Dansereau, Arthur, et al. **George-Étienne Cartier, Études. Edition du centenaire 1814-1914.** Montréal: Librairie Beauchemin Limitée, 1914. (Numerous primary source quotes)

den Otter, A.A. **Civilizing the West: The Galts and the Development of Western Canada.** Edmonton: The University of Alberta Press, 1982.

Evans, A. Margaret. **Sir Oliver Mowat. The Ontario Historical Studies Series.** Toronto: University of Toronto Press, 1992.

Hannay, James. **The Life and Times of Sir Leonard Tilley, Being a Political History of New Brunswick for the Last Seventy Years.** St. John, N.B., 1897. (Many primary source citations)

Hardy, W.G. **From Sea Unto Sea; the Road to Nationhood, 1850-1910. Vol. 4, Canadian History Series**, ed. by Thomas B. Costain. Toronto: Doubleday Canada Limited, 1970.

Lewis, John. **George Brown. The Makers of Canada.** Toronto: Morang & Col, Ltd.,1906. (Numerous primary source citations)

Phelan, Josephine. **The Ardent Exile, the Life and Times of Thomas D'Arcy McGee.** Toronto: The Macmillan Company of Canada, 1951.

Skelton, Oscar Douglas. **Life and Times of Alexander Tilloch Galt. Carleton Library, No. 26.** Toronto: McClelland and Stewart, 1966.

Made in the USA
Middletown, DE
29 February 2020